Education
and the employment problem
in developing countries

Mark Blaug

Education
and the employment problem
in developing countries

International Labour Office   Geneva

ISBN 92-2-101005-8

First published 1973

Second impression 1974

PRINTED BY IMPRIMERIE LA CONCORDE, LAUSANNE (SWITZERLAND)

PREFACE

The International Development Strategy of the Second Development Decade places a heavy emphasis on employment as a major goal of development policies. In specific terms, the Strategy suggests that "each developing country should formulate its national employment objectives so as to absorb an increasing proportion of its working population in modern-type activities and to reduce significantly unemployment and underemployment". The World Employment Programme, launched officially in 1969, represents the contribution of the International Labour Organisation to the Strategy of the Second Development Decade. The aim of the World Employment Programme is to provide national policy-makers and planners with practical guidelines that will enable them to accelerate the rate of growth of productive employment.

The following activities have recently been undertaken to give practical effect to the objectives of the World Employment Programme. First, a major research programme has been launched in seven areas, namely : population growth ; choice of techniques ; income distribution ; educational policies ; trade policies ; urban employment problems ; and emergency employment schemes.[1] Second, comprehensive employment strategy missions have been sent to Colombia, Iran, Kenya and Sri Lanka[2] and additional missions to other

[1] These projects are fully described in ILO : *Scope, approach and content of research-oriented activities of the World Employment Programme* (Geneva, 1972).

[2] See :
Idem : *Towards full employment : a programme for Colombia* (Geneva, 1970) ;
Idem : *Employment and incomes policies for Iran* (Geneva, 1973) ;
Idem : *Employment, incomes and equality : a strategy for increasing productive employment in Kenya* (Geneva, 1972) ;
Idem : *Matching employment opportunities and expectations : a programme of action for Ceylon* (Geneva, 1971), 2 vols.
At the time when the comprehensive employment strategy mission to Sri Lanka took place, that country was still known as Ceylon and the mission's report became generally known as the "Ceylon report". This designation is retained throughout this book. The other three mission reports listed above are similarly referred to hereafter as the Colombia, Iran and Kenya reports.

countries are now being planned. Third, regional employment teams have been established in Latin America and Asia and several subregional teams are now being constituted in Africa. Fourth, a number of independent scholars have been commissioned to study special aspects of the employment problem in less developed countries in an effort to promote the widest possible discussion of the relevant issues.

The present work, forming part of the World Employment Programme's project on education, the labour market and employment financed by the Danish International Development Agency (DANIDA), is an example of these independent studies.[1] Its principal aim is to assess the responsibility of the educational authorities in the employment problem of less developed countries. Are there reasons to think that the quantity and quality of education in a country make a significant impact on the employment problem of less developed countries ? If so, how can educational systems be reformed so as to maximise the rate of growth of income-earning opportunities ? Which policies are actually feasible in the light of different national conditions ? These are the sort of questions to which this monograph is addressed.

The subject is a controversial one and the author speaks for himself, not for the ILO. Indeed, much of his analysis proceeds by way of a critical commentary of some of the ideas contained in the four comprehensive employment strategy mission reports that the ILO has already published. The conclusions reached in this study are at best tentative : far too little is known about some of the key relationships to allow one to draw definite conclusions. It is precisely for this reason that the World Employment Programme contains a generous dose of research-oriented activities.

People, acting as individuals, parents, members of groups from communities to national governments, have multiple and complex expectations for education. The effects of education on employment and economic growth and vice versa are only a part of the larger pattern so aptly described by the title of the report of the International Commission for the Development of Education *Learning to be*.[2] For "the aim of development is the complete fulfilment of man, in all the richness of his personality, the complexity of his forms of expression and his various commitments—as individual, member of a family and of a community, citizen and producer, inventor of techniques and creative dreamer". [3]

---

[1] See also Paul Bairoch : *Urban unemployment in developing countries* (Geneva, ILO, 1973).

[2] Edgar Faure *et al.* : *Learning to be* (Paris, Unesco ; London, Harrap, 1972).

[3] Ibid., p. vi.

CONTENTS

THE EMPLOYMENT PROBLEM

1

In one sense it is all too easy to explain why the less developed countries suffer from an apparently chronic problem of mass unemployment. The conjunction of unusually high rates of population growth, extremely low rates of capital accumulation and imperfect factor substitutability suffice to account for the phenomenon in general terms. Rates of population growth are unusually high in these countries because advances in medicine brought about a reduction in the death rate long before family planning began to affect the birth rate. On the other hand, rates of capital accumulation are extremely low because poor societies find it difficult to save a large fraction of their income and because the rich who are the savers tend for a variety of reasons to speculate in real estate rather than to invest in productive capacity. Factor substitutability is imperfect because modern technology is capital-intensive; although the handling of materials and the distribution of the final product offer scope for a more generous use of labour than is customary in industrialised countries the result is nevertheless an over-all ratio of capital to labour that is too high to achieve full employment. Besides, a wage rate so low as to absorb all labour into employment, assuming this were technically possible by the development of labour-intensive "intermediate technology", would fall below the subsistence wage rate and would therefore achieve full employment at the cost of mass starvation. Thus, less developed countries are bound to suffer from what Joan Robinson has called "Marxian unemployment" as distinct from "Keynesian unemployment": it is not lack of aggregate demand but lack of capital in relation to the size of the labour force that basically accounts for mass unemployment in the Third World.

Nevertheless, the less developed countries enjoyed impressive growth rates in the 1950s and 1960s, which ought to have reduced their unemployment problem. In point of fact, however, the problem seems in some respects to have become more serious. In recent years, open unemployment in urban areas has reached percentage rates such as 13.6 in Colombia and 7.9 in Venezuela ; 9.8 in Malaysia, 11.6 in the Philippines and 15.0 in Sri Lanka ; 11.6 in Ghana and 14.9 in Kenya.[1] Whatever the facts, there is a widespread impression that rates as high as these were not experienced in the past. Similarly, the average level of education of the unemployed appears to have risen sharply in recent years. In Tropical Africa there is now almost certainly mass unemployment among primary school leavers, and heavy unemployment among secondary school graduates has recently become a familiar feature of many countries in Asia and Latin America. All this has given rise to the conviction that there is something wrong with the pattern of economic growth in less developed countries : incomes per head growing at rates as high as 3 to 4 per cent are apparently compatible with the continued existence of 10 per cent unemployment rates. It is this conviction that gave rise in the late 1960s to the notion of an employment-oriented development strategy for less developed countries and in 1969 to the creation of the ILO's World Employment Programme.

UNEMPLOYMENT OR POVERTY ?

The World Employment Programme's main objective was originally to persuade developing countries and international donors to make maximum feasible employment a central goal of economic policy. It is probably true to say that this objective has now been replaced by one which seeks to emphasise poverty as the crucial problem of economic development. The original aim was well expressed by David A. Morse, the Director-General of the ILO in 1968.[2] Subsequent discussions between ILO officials and international experts led to a wider interpretation of the concept of an employment-oriented development strategy[3], and the current doctrine emerged in clear outline in the Colombia report, relating to the first of the ILO's comprehensive employment strategy missions.[4]

The central theme of the Colombia report is that the main problem is not so much open unemployment, or even underemployment, but rather the type of gainful employment provided for many of those actually at work. The so-called "employment problem" is primarily a problem of inadequate

---

[1] See David Turnham (assisted by Ingelies Jaeger) : *The employment problem in less developed countries : a review of evidence* (Paris, OECD Development Centre, 1971).

[2] David A. Morse : "The World Employment Programme", in *International Labour Review* (Geneva, ILO), Vol. 97, No. 6, June 1968.

[3] See W. Arthur Lewis : "Summary : the causes of unemployment in less developed countries and some research topics", ibid., Vol. 101, No. 5, May 1970.

[4] For a succinct summary of the report by the Chief of the Mission, Dudley Seers, see his "New approaches suggested by the Colombia employment programme", in Walter Galenson (ed.) : *Essays on employment* (Geneva, ILO, 1971).

income and only secondarily one of insufficient work opportunities. In consequence, the ultimate object of policy is not just to provide more jobs but to
provide more jobs of the sort that yield enough income to sustain a reasonable
standard of living.

The point is familiar to those who have kept up with the interminable
debate over the last 20 years about the question of how best to measure unemployment in less developed countries. The simplest approach is to count
everybody without work who is actually seeking employment at going wage
rates in the "reference week"; this is the standard definition of "visible unemployment". Unfortunately, persistently high rates of unemployment are
likely to cause people to stop looking for work. A certain volume of "visible
unemployment" may therefore be attended with a much larger volume of
"invisible unemployment", which is virtually impossible to measure. At any
rate, if chronic open unemployment in developing countries tends steadily
to reduce their labour force participation rates, the result is to impart a constant downward bias to their reported rates of visible unemployment.

If this were not bad enough, we have the further problem of "visible and
invisible underemployment", in the sense of employed people who would
like to work longer hours in order to earn more, whether they actually seek
a job with longer hours or not. This problem of part-time work is a pervasive
phenomenon in less developed countries, largely because of the absence of
unemployment compensation schemes. In these countries people are, as it
were, too poor to afford the "luxury" of unemployment on a full-time basis.
Hence they accept some work, however little, in preference to none. The
result is that the distribution of employment by hours worked per week,
which in developed countries is virtually a discontinuous function at 40-
45 hours per week, is in less developed countries a fairly smooth continuous
function from zero to 50 or even 60 hours a week.[1]

---

[1] The argument is illustrated by the following representative diagram:

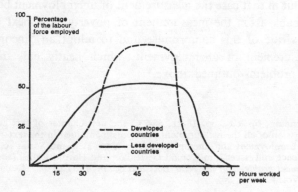

What this means is that we cannot measure unemployment without in fact including some underemployment, and we cannot measure either unambiguously because we first have to decide who should be included in the labour force, which itself depends on the level of unemployment. One might go so far as to say that the problem of defining employment and unemployment in less developed countries is very similar to committing Type I and Type II errors in the Fisher-Neyman theory of statistical inference : if one is made larger, the other is necessarily made smaller. If we define "employment" as working at least one eight-hour day in the reference week and "unemployment" as seeking at least one day's work at going wage rates—the Indian definition—we get a large number for employment and therefore a small number for unemployment : to be unemployed now means that you do not even work one day a week but the millions who work only two days are counted as employed ! If instead we define "employment" as working at least 20 hours a week, we get a small number for employment but a large number for unemployment : people will be counted as unemployed even if they work two days a week ! In that sense, a country can make its unemployment rate anything it likes by suitably defining the numerator of the unemployment rate.

The problem of definition is still further confused by the two senses in which economists have spoken of "underemployment". We have defined it just now as a situation in which some people who are working would in fact like to work longer hours. Presumably, the only way in which this could conceivably be measured is by means of attitude surveys. But another definition of "underemployment" is that of people, working both part time and full time, who are not efficiently utilised ; that is, they could produce more if the job in which they are employed were differently organised. This is a "productivity" definition of underemployment which may give quite different results from an "attitudinal" definition. Since the productivity of individuals cannot be directly measured, attempts have been made to measure it indirectly via income payments. But in that case the measurement of unemployment becomes almost indistinguishable from the measurement of poverty. The next step is indeed to make a virtue of this compromise and to adopt an "income approach" to the measurement of unemployment, which neatly cuts through all the definitional problems outlined above.[1]

---

[1] See Turnham, op. cit., pp. 18-21, 68-71 ; the first chapter of this book provides an excellent discussion of all the measurement problems mentioned in the text. See also Ronald G. Ridker : "Employment and unemployment in Near East and South Asian countries : a review of evidence and issues", in Ronald G. Ridker and Harold Lubell (eds.) : *Employment and unemployment problems of the Near East and South Asia*, 2 vols. (Delhi, Vikas Publications, 1971), Vol. I.

The Colombia report in fact proposes to define the "employment problem" in terms of inadequate incomes : people who are either employed or unemployed but who are in any case receiving a lower income than is required to provide what is judged to be a "minimum standard of living" in that country. It is clear that this definition includes the whole of what others have called "visible and invisible unemployment", but it is not clear whether it would also include the whole of "underemployment", defined either in terms of lower hours than people would like to work or in terms of lower productivity than is technically possible, although it certainly includes part of it.[1]

The following bar-chart sums up the argument.

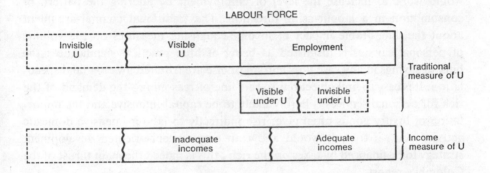

THE COLOMBIA REPORT

The income approach to the measurement of unemployment is clearly more comprehensive than the traditional definition of open unemployment plus underemployment. The result of adopting the comprehensive definition is that the treatment of the nature of the employment problem must become equally comprehensive, amounting in fact to an analysis of all the factors that keep certain countries poor. Nevertheless, the Colombia report gives prominence to certain key elements in the situation.

First of all, it emphasises the role of artificial factor prices in lowering the volume of employment in Colombia: an overvalued exchange rate, coupled with a system of import quotas and subsidised interest rates, has reduced the price of capital, while an elaborate system of labour laws has raised the real price of labour to employers. Similarly, it lays stress on the fact that the capacity of agriculture to absorb additional numbers into employment has

---

[1] The basic statement of the dimensions of the "employment problem" mentions "under-utilisation" as one of the elements, as distinct from and possibly in addition to "inadequate incomes" (Colombia report, p. 15). See also the equally ambiguous statement in the Ceylon report, pp. 19-20.

been held back by the failure to break up large estates and to promote family farming. Lastly, and more controversially, it establishes a direct link between the employment problem and the highly unequal distribution of income that characterises Colombia along with almost all other developing countries. The link is forged in a traditional Ricardian manner by way of the typical spending patterns of rich and poor consumers. The contention is that the goods that are widely purchased by the poor are largely produced at home by relatively labour-intensive methods (food, clothing, footwear, and so on), while the rich tend to buy imported goods or domestically produced goods with a low direct-labour content. For that reason, a more equal distribution of income would work to increase the level of employment by altering the pattern of consumption in a labour-using direction. The traditional counter-argument about the undesirable impact of income-equalising measures on the volume of personal savings is dismissed as being of little practical significance: the bulk of savings in any case flow abroad or else are frittered away in land speculation. It is easy to find objections to this line of reasoning—the demand of the rich for personal services is hardly likely to be capital-intensive and the importation of luxury goods often gives rise indirectly to labour-intensive domestic activity—but, if true, it would allow an employment-oriented development strategy to be financed by taxes on the rich ; this is indeed the main thrust of the Colombia report.

The Colombia report lays down the basic target of 5 million jobs by 1985 and calculates output and employment paths for the different sectors of the Colombian economy to achieve this objective. Oddly enough, however, it combines an employment target (an increase in the growth of employment from 5.2 per cent experienced in 1964-70 to 8.1 per cent over the years 1970-85) with a more ambitious output target than has previously been achieved or planned for in Colombia. In this sense, it gains the employment objective without surrendering the output objective.

And why not ? The maximisation of employment may conflict with the maximisation of output, but there is no inherent reason why it should do so. At the risk of over-simplification, we might say that policies designed to maximise employment are compatible with policies that will maximise output if the adoption of a more all-round labour-intensive technology is at the same time also capital-saving. Unless this is true, it will prove impossible to finance rising capital requirements per unit of output out of domestic savings ; to do so out of international borrowing is effective only if exports can be made perpetually to grow faster than imports. In short, there may be a trade-off between employment and output objectives ; but on the other hand the dilemma is avoidable and clearly has been effectively avoided by such countries as Japan and the Republic of Korea.

Besides, the conflict between employment and output objectives is not so much an issue of fact as of social choice. The conflict ultimately reduces to one of jobs now or jobs later because more output today promotes more jobs tomorrow. Since the choice is one of different time paths of output and hence of employment, the answer must involve social time preferences for both output and employment.[1] Be that as it may, it is perfectly conceivable that the same rate of economic growth may be accompanied by a higher or lower volume of employment depending on the structure of the growth path of an economy. Admittedly, it is easier to seize on key factors that produce a high growth rate with little extra employment (for example, a policy of import substitution which protects nascent industry) than to spell out the precise pattern of economic growth that will secure the maximum volume of employment. The Colombia report frankly acknowledges the unsatisfactory state of current knowledge about these questions :

> The basic choice of strategy is how much reliance to put on different sectors as job providers. [...] A major difficulty for those tackling this question is that it is not one on which the traditional tools of economic analysis are very helpful. Appropriate models have not yet been devised to show the effects of the interaction of employment, productivity, investment and output in different sectors, let alone how movements in these key variables, especially during the approach to full employment, affect relative prices of factors or products, and thus the distribution of income, or how these changes in prices in turn influence the patterns of growth. Nor has enough research been done even to provide the basis for selecting the type of model most appropriate.[2]

EDUCATED UNEMPLOYMENT

The accent on poverty, on the redistribution of the gains from economic growth rather than on employment promotion as such, is consistently maintained in the ILO mission reports for Iran, Kenya and Sri Lanka. The Ceylon report once again returns to distorted factor prices and unequal incomes as the principal causes of the employment problem, attaching particular significance to the relatively large differentials between skilled and unskilled labour that prevail in the labour markets of Sri Lanka. What stands out in the Kenya report, on the other hand, is the emphasis on the employment potential of the so-called "unorganised" sector of the Kenyan economy : the vast proliferation of small enterprises employing not more than 10 workers, using labour-intensive techniques to manufacture most of the non-agricultural goods consumed by the poor. The Kenya report accepts the fact that an employment

---

[1] For a full discussion, see Frances Stewart and Paul Streeten : "Conflicts between output and employment objectives in developing countries", in *Oxford Economic Papers* (London), Vol. 23, No. 2, July 1971, pp. 145-168.

[2] Colombia report, p. 51.

strategy may conflict with an output strategy, and for the first time sets minimum household target incomes for 1978 and 1985 as having overriding priority in economic planning.

Although the Colombia report makes only incidental references to educated unemployment [1], this topic looms large in both the Ceylon and the Kenya reports. In Sri Lanka the problem is largely, although not exclusively, one of unemployment among secondary school leavers. In Kenya, on the other hand, it is the primary school leavers who constitute the bulk of the unemployed. Both reports take the view that the problem of educated unemployment is essentially one of mismatch between the job expectations generated by the traditional educational system and the job opportunities provided by the labour market : to cut down the output of primary and secondary schools or to somehow expand jobs, while leaving the structure of wages, salaries and fringe benefits what it is, will not in fact solve anything. Both reports, therefore, propose to deal with the problem by a combined attack on the content of formal education and on the structure of monetary incentives provided by the labour market. In the language of the Kenya report :

The school leaver problem in Kenya is more complex than is often assumed. It is an over-simplification to consider it essentially as an excess of new school leavers over new job openings for which their educational qualifications are required. [. . .] The root of the problem lies in the interaction of the conventional educational system and the wage and salary structure through the allocation of jobs and wages by reference primarily to educational qualifications.[2]

And again, in the words of an ILO official :

It is obvious that education is in no way responsible for the problem of *over-all* imbalance (i.e. between labour supply and demand). Changes in the educational system will not change the number of job opportunities in the economy (except to the extent that changes in pupil-teacher ratios affect the demand for teaching staff). However, education is definitely responsible for one of the problems of *structural* imbalance : that of matching employment opportunities and expectations. This is one of the lessons to be drawn from the Colombia and Ceylon employment reports, in particular the latter.[3]

Here indeed is the central question with which we are concerned : are the educational authorities in fact responsible for "one of the problems of structural imbalance", while being utterly blameless for "the problem of over-all imbalance" ? The answer to this question will take many pages, but by way of clearing the ground we have a question of fact to settle at the outset : can we believe the mounting evidence that the highest rates of visible unemployment

---

[1] The Colombia report admits, however, that "there is at present no general shortage of persons with middle or higher levels of education. Indeed, at university level there is some evidence that the recent rapid expansion may have exceeded economic needs" (pp. 225-227).

[2] Kenya report, pp. 10-11.

[3] Louis Emmerij : "Research priorities of the World Employment Programme", in *International Labour Review*, Vol. 105, No. 5, May 1972, p. 415.

in less developed countries are to be found among those with secondary rather than with primary education ? If we can, it will prove difficult to deny the argument that additional schooling aggravates the employment problem by somehow generating unrealistic expectations.

If we graph the rate of unemployment among those who have completed successively higher levels of education against the levels themselves, we may find : (1) [a negative relationship—more education appears to improve the chances of employment ; (2) a positive relationship—more education appears to make people less employable ; or (3) an inverted U-shape, exemplifying the finding mentioned above that the rate of unemployment for secondary school graduates exceeds that of primary school leavers, although it declines again for university graduates. The Ceylon and Iran reports found evidence of this inverted U-curve [1], but the Colombia and Kenya reports instead found support for the negative relationship, the unemployment rate being worst among those with no education whatsoever.[2] The inverted U-curve has also been observed in Argentina, India, Malaysia, Syria and Venezuela [3] ; but in the Philippines the rate of unemployment by education has again been shown to decline monotonically with additional years of schooling.[4] The evidence is therefore confused and the U-shaped pattern is by no means wel established as the general case.

Even if it were, I doubt that it would tell us very much about the effects of education on employment prospects. The fact is that a cross-section observation of rates of unemployment by years of schooling is the outcome of a number of conflicting forces which confuse interpretation of the data. Firstly, labour force participation rates are in most countries positively related to educational attainment. This factor alone, everything else being the same, will produce a tendency for the unemployment *rate* to decline with levels of education, simply because the denominator of the unemployment rate rises with higher and higher levels of education. But everything else is not the same : if the educational system is growing very rapidly, students will constitute a rising percentage of the labour force as time passes. If the upper levels of the educa-

---

[1] Ceylon report, pp. 3, 28-29, 132 ; Iran report, Vol. B, App. I, p. 6 (mimeographed).

[2] Colombia report, p. 358 ; Kenya report, p. 59, tables 18 and 19.

[3] Turnham, op. cit., pp. 51-52. See also Mark Blaug, Richard Layard and Maureen Woodhall : *The causes of graduate unemployment in India* (London, Allen Lane The Penguin Press, 1969), pp. 63-64. Some countries report evidence both for drop-outs and for those who complete a level, in which case the pattern takes on a zigzag form. In Peru, for example, the rate of educated unemployment in 1970 was highest for those with incomplete secondary education ; it fell for those with completed secondary education and then rose again for university graduates (*Informe sobre la situación ocupacional del Perú* (Lima, Ministerio del Trabajo, Servicio del Empleo y Recursos Humanos, 1971), p. II - 13).

[4] Mark Blaug : "Educated unemployment in Asia : a contrast between India and the Philippines", in *Philippine Economic Journal* (Manila), Fall 1972.

tional system are growing more rapidly than the lower levels, as in practically all less developed countries, this tends further to reduce the rate of educated unemployment. So far, we have two reasons for a negative relationship between the unemployment rate and years of schooling. But the effect of population growth easily outweighs the influence of all the other factors. A population growing at 3 per cent or more may have an age distribution in which half of the population is 15 years old or younger and 60 per cent is less than 25 years old. If the labour market is poorly organised, or if employers are rightly or wrongly unwilling to hire youngsters, so that in the best of circumstances it takes a graduate several months to find suitable work, the rate of educated unemployment is almost bound to be higher than that of unemployment in general. In that case, educated people are unemployed not because they are educated but because they are young and inexperienced. Indeed, we may go further and say that so long as even a perfectly competitive labour market does not respond instantaneously, a sustained expansion of education at an accelerated rate will necessarily result in relatively high rates of educated unemployment for long periods of time. Most of the less developed countries have in fact experienced rising enrolment rates, particularly in secondary and higher education, over the last 10 or 15 years. No wonder then that they suffer from educated unemployment. In short, the figures that are usually cited prove nothing as such about the causes of educated unemployment.

Thus, in the Philippines, a general unemployment rate of 8 per cent in 1965 is combined with rates of 55 per cent for those with some completed primary education, 26 per cent for those with high school education and 13 per cent for those with college education. This seems to suggest that education makes unemployment worse, until we notice that over half of all those who are unemployed are aged 25 years or less and are still looking for their first regular job ; indeed, one-third of the unemployed are less than 20 years old.[1] Educated unemployment in the Philippines therefore is practically the same problem as youth unemployment.

It is clear from considerations such as these that relevant evidence is not the rate of open unemployment among particular categories of people but rather the waiting period before entering a job, or the average duration of unemployment. There is a world of difference between a situation in which everybody takes six months to find a job and then holds on to it until retirement and one where 90 per cent find work on the day they leave school, while 10 per cent take five years to get a job, although both situations actually yield identical unemployment rates. Thus, it is more illuminating to be told,

---

[1] Similar figures for Colombia are found in the Colombia report, pp. 27, 357-358 ; see also Turnham, op. cit., pp. 47-50.

not that educated unemployment among high school and college graduates in India in 1967 was about 15 per cent of the economically active stock of educated labour but rather that the "average waiting time" of high school graduates was 18 months, while the "average waiting time" of college graduates was six months.[1] Unfortunately, India is unique among the developing countries in providing this kind of information.

I think it is fair to conclude that data on unemployment in less developed countries are worth little unless they are cross-classified by age, education and the duration of unemployment ; but more important than all these is the entire distribution of employment and unemployment by hours worked per week. Since this evidence is, to my knowledge, unavailable for any developing country, there is little point in quibbling about unemployment statistics. All the figures are high in comparison to advanced countries, and that will suffice for present purposes.

THE QUESTION OF RESPONSIBILITY

Enough has now been said to suggest that the "employment problem" in less developed countries is really a series of overlapping problems related to : (1) visible unemployment ; (2) invisible unemployment ; (3) underemployment (in the sense of unutilised productive potential) ; (4) school leaver unemployment (unemployment among those with no more than primary education) ; (5) educated unemployment (unemployment among those with at least some secondary education) ; (6) youth unemployment ; and (7) the working poor. When we ask : "What is the responsibility of the educational authorities in the 'employment problem' of less developed countries ?" the answer clearly depends on which aspect of the problem we have in mind. Earlier we cited one commentator who denied the responsibility of education in creating or perpetuating either visible or invisible unemployment but who affirmed this responsibility in the case of school leaver and educated unemployment. But others might argue, and many have argued, that education is at least in part responsible for the whole problem of open and disguised unemployment, claiming that the bulk of existing formal education in less developed countries restricts children's initiative and thus stunts the entrepreneurial spirit, or at any rate discourages them from taking up self-employment which might in turn create jobs for others. Expressed more mildly, the thesis runs : education may not create the over-all surplus of labour but once it exists it does nothing to alleviate it and probably makes it worse. A variation of this argument is the widely held view that education in developing countries promotes

[1] Blaug, Layard and Woodhall, op. cit., pp. 75-81, 89-90.

the flight from farming and the rush to urban centres and in this way tends to convert disguised rural unemployment and underemployment into open urban unemployment. This is to say that education may not cause unemployment but it certainly tends to bring it to the surface.[1] Besides, there is the fact that education absorbs funds that might have been devoted to the direct creation of jobs. In that sense, the educational authorities, whatever they do, cannot fail to make an impact on the "employment problem".

All this says nothing yet about the working poor who, as we noted earlier, are at the heart of the "employment problem" of less developed countries as the World Employment Programme conceives it. But are the educational authorities responsible for the existence of poverty? No, if we mean that poverty would be reduced if only the educational system would quietly disappear. But yes, if we can think of some educational reforms that might, in conjunction with other measures, make an impact on the poverty problem; and definitely yes, if there are educational policies that can, by themselves, affect the hiring standards of the working poor. The answer depends crucially on what is meant by "responsibility"; in other words, on the closeness of the link between education and the problem in question. Poverty is apparently a problem that is only indirectly affected by education and then only in the longest of long runs. Education may "cause" economic growth but the effect shows up first among those who have received additional schooling and only much later among the poor who largely missed these opportunities. There is scope here for educational policy, but only if the policy is an integral feature of a general development strategy. Open unemployment is perhaps more closely linked than is poverty to the quantity and quality of schooling in a society, but nevertheless even here the chain of causation is a lengthy one, requiring decades and even generations to work itself out. A long-run employment-oriented development strategy ought to contain proposals for reforming the educational system but perhaps it would not be fatally marred if it contained none—this will turn out to be the principal bone of contention in this area! The same is true, I think, of disguised unemployment; but when we come to school leaver unemployment and educated unemployment the responsibility of the educational authorities is perfectly clear. Even if nothing else changed, it is possible to think of educational reforms that would almost immediately affect the magnitude and incidence of unemployment among the young and the relatively well educated.

It is often said that educational reforms without complementary action in other areas would achieve nothing. But of course the same thing is also being

---

[1] Indeed, urban rates of open unemployment are generally higher than rural rates (Turnham, op. cit., p. 43), probably because work sharing is more difficult to organise in towns.

said of changes in these other areas. When a manpower planner proposes a a new scheme of vocational counselling, he will usually warn that the scheme will come to nothing unless it is accompanied by specific changes in the curricula of schools. When a public health expert advocates a new programme to improve village wells, he will note that the programme depends for its effectiveness on concomitant changes in rural education and agricultural extension. Everything depends on everything else. Hence the need for a general development strategy.

All this is very true, and yet it is not quite true. There *are* spheres of relative autonomy ; if this were not so, piecemeal improvement in any one direction would be doomed at the start. It is evident that the doctrine of general interdependence—everything depends on everything else—can become a perfect excuse for doing nothing. Even the perfectly integrated development plan cannot ensure that all ministries will launch their programmes at precisely the same moment. If every ministry waits on every other to get started, nothing ever happens. We must therefore rank the responsibilities of ministries in the solution of some outstanding problem in terms of the degree of impact which ministerial action taken by itself is likely to have on the problem at hand. Otherwise, the question of responsibility turns into one of participation in the development plan, which is true but not very helpful.

I have just argued that the educational authorities have a more immediate responsibility for youth unemployment than for general unemployment, underemployment and poverty. That may or may not be true, but at least it begins to introduce the kind of distinctions which will prove helpful in sorting out the variety of educational policies that have been advocated at one time or another in relation to the "employment problem" of less developed countries. In later chapters, we shall be asking whether such things as curriculum reform, abolition of examinations, vocationalisation of secondary schools, quantitative controls on enrolments, increases in school fees, recurrent education, out-of-school training schemes and functional literacy programmes could alleviate the "employment problem". We now see that it all depends on which aspect of the "employment problem" we have in mind, and particularly on whether we want quick results or whether we are willing patiently to pin our hopes on the long run.

LESSONS FROM THE ECONOMICS OF EDUCATION

2

The economics of education is a young subject : it emerged as a separate branch of economics only some 10 to 15 years ago. It would be surprising, therefore, if it were now capable of furnishing clear, practical advice to educational planners in less developed countries. Nevertheless, it is evident that much of the research in this field has been inspired by the hope of providing answers to policy questions, and it is also evident that the drift of this research tends to support certain policy positions and to undermine others. In this chapter we shall derive some of the practical guidelines that have emerged from recent work in the economics of education, and these will serve, together with the next chapter, as background material for the discussion of solutions to the "employment problem".

THE OPTIMUM SHAPE OF THE EDUCATIONAL PYRAMID

The most striking presumption to emerge from the burgeoning literature in the economics of education is that almost all less developed countries suffer from persistent underinvestment in primary education, hand-in-hand with persistent overinvestment in higher education. Ever since 1950 or thereabouts, higher education has been the fastest-growing part of the educational system the world over, whether measured in terms of enrolments or in terms of financial outlay. In the 1950s and early 1960s, the principal rationale for the rapid expansion of higher education was manpower forecasting : all the long-term manpower forecasts in Africa, Asia and Latin America foresaw an enormous shortage of secondary and higher educated manpower. In the last few years, however, a sense of disillusionment with manpower forecasting has gradually spread through the world, in part because it implies an over-rigid view of the capacity of the economic system to absorb educated people into employment, and in part because of a growing fear that it constitutes an open-ended invitation to expand secondary and higher education without limits. Perhaps more important than either of these considerations is the realisation that manpower forecasting leaves the educational planner with virtually no choices to make. Since the forecasting methods employed are generally acknowledged to be inapplicable to the so-called "requirements" for primary-educated workers (these largely end up in family farming) and since the costs of education do not influence the final results of the exercise, the typical manpower forecast necessarily commits the bulk of educational expenditures to the expansion of secondary and higher education. It is only after this first call on public funds is met that the educational planner can start thinking about such alternatives as quantitative expansion versus qualitative improvements, formal education in schools versus informal on-the-job training, and adult literacy versus schooling for children; but on all these questions he gets no help from manpower forecasts.

. In retrospect, it is easy to see why manpower forecasting enjoyed such popularity, and its intuitive appeal is such that it will probably endure for many years to come, for the mounting evidence that an extraordinary variety of manpower structures are compatible with identical levels and rates of growth of national income has still not been adequately assimilated.[1] Similarly, there has been some reluctance to accept the limited ability of economists to forecast the economic future accurately. Because of the length of most educational cycles, manpower forecasts that attempt to be useful to educational planning are impelled to look ahead at least five to ten years. Of course, no one is surprised to discover that completely accurate forecasting is impossible over such lengths of time; but what is disturbing is that virtually all manpower forecasts of the long-term variety have turned out to be seriously wrong.[2] Fairly accurate predictions can be made for two- to three-year periods, and these are undoubtedly useful for an "active manpower policy" that provides information for training programmes, labour placement services, vocational guidance, and the like. In time, by continuously evaluating the short-term forecasts, we shall undoubtedly learn to predict better in the medium and

---

[1] Some of this evidence is to be found in Robinson Hollister: *A technical evaluation of the first stage of the Mediterranean Regional Project* (Paris, OECD, 1967), and OECD: *Occupational and educational structures of the labour force and levels of economic development* (Paris, 1970). It is further discussed in my *Introduction to the economics of education* (London, Penguin Books, 1970), Ch. 5.

[2] See Bashir Ahamad and Mark Blaug (eds.): *The practice of manpower forecasting: a collection of case studies* (Amsterdam, Elsevier Scientific Publishing Co., 1973), which consists, among other things, of a detailed appraisal of the forecasting experience of eight countries, of which three are less developed countries (India, Nigeria and Thailand). See also Richard Jolly and Christopher Colclough: "African manpower plans: an evaluation", in *International Labour Review*, Vol. 106, Nos. 2-3, Aug.-Sep. 1972, in which equally severe but less extreme conclusions are reached.

long term. But over the next decade or so there will be little point in arguing whether educational systems should be geared to long-term manpower requirements, because experience has shown that they cannot be.

There are, however, other ways of carrying out educational planning, even when we are concerned only with narrow economic objectives. The leading alternative approach is cost-benefit analysis, sometimes labelled rate-of-return analysis. This too has obvious deficiencies, but it does have the merit of getting us started on the right foot : when we decide to spend another dollar on education rather than on some other activity, or on one kind of education rather than another, we do so in the belief that, for a given outlay, some stated goal can be more effectively achieved ; when the goal is an economic one, we must be saying in effect that the contemplated action will result in greater economic benefits per unit of costs than any other. Cost-benefit analysis, therefore, is surely the appropriate framework for thinking about educational planning for economic ends ?

In practice, the benefits of education in rate-of-return analysis are taken to be the extra earnings that typically accrue to people with additional education after standardising for differences in family background and, where possible, native ability measured at an early age. In countries where there is a significant amount of unemployment, the data are usually adjusted for the average chance of finding work at various levels of educational achievement. No allowance is made, however, for the so-called "externalities" or "neighbourhood effects" of education nor for its intrinsic value, none of which are reflected in personal income flows. This is a serious objection, however, only if we are making ambitious comparisons between expenditures on education and expenditures on, say, health or transport ; it is much less of a problem when we are comparing expenditures between different levels of education, unless of course we have reason to know that, for example, higher education generates more externalities than secondary education. We know very little about the externalities of education and there is not even agreement among economists as to what form they take.[1] It would be a bold planner, therefore, who could claim that certain levels of the educational system generate greater neighbourhood effects than others. It does, however, come back to plague us when we are comparing different types of education at the same level, as, for example, academic secondary versus vocational secondary schools or the study of medicine versus the study of literature in universities.

---

[1] The question is often confused with the social, cultural and political benefits of education. Apart from higher earnings, it is said, more education also contributes to equality of opportunity, national integration, and so on. Are not these "externalities" of education ? No, not in the technical sense of the term. These are different objectives for education. Cost-benefit analysis, it must be emphasised, is concerned only with economic objectives.

A deeper question is whether the higher earnings of better-educated people really reflect their superior contribution to national income, a question we shall explore at length in the next chapter. All we need to say here is that if the structure of wages and salaries in an economy is a matter merely of social conventions, it will affect the price of steel as much as it does the economic returns to education ; yet few planners would use such an argument to deny the value of calculating the expected rate of return on a new steel factory before constructing it. In other words, if true, it spoils the case not just for cost-benefit analysis of education but for all project appraisals that involve the use of observed prices. It is perfectly true, however, that the rate of return on educational investment in a country is a meaningless statistic if the pattern of earnings bears no relationship whatsoever to the relative scarcities of people with different skills. For that reason, rate-of-return studies in less developed countries increasingly link their calculations to an analysis of the operations of the labour market.[1] To sum up : a rate-of-return calculation only creates a presumption of how resources ought to be reallocated within the educational system ; it cannot by itself prove that they are misallocated.

With these caveats, we can now ask what rate-of-return analysis reveals about investment in different levels of education in the Third World. We have relevant data for 18 countries, of which 10 are less developed countries, and in most of these (Brazil, Malaysia and the Philippines are exceptions) primary education yields higher social rates of return than any other level of education.[2] As between secondary and higher education, however, the situation is more mixed : in half of the less developed countries, secondary education also ranks above higher education, but in the other half the ranking is reversed. Nevertheless, on average, the social rate of return on secondary education in less developed countries exceeds that on higher education (see table 1).

The one general lesson we can draw from these results, therefore, is that there appears to be underinvestment in primary education in almost all less developed countries ; that is to say, given the existing quality of education, too much is being spent on the higher levels and too little on the lower levels of the system. I must emphasise the fact that this is a conclusion about quantities : rate-of-return data cannot tell us what would happen if the content of primary schooling were radically altered [3] ; they cannot even tell us how far to

---

[1] See, for example, Hans Heinrich Thias and Martin Carnoy : *Cost-benefit analysis in education : a case study of Kenya* (Washington, DC, International Bank for Reconstruction and Development, 1972) ; and Blaug, Layard and Woodhall, op. cit.

[2] George Psacharopoulos : *The economic returns to education in the process of development : an international comparison* (Amsterdam, Elsevier Scientific Publishing Co., 1972), Ch. 4. See also idem : "Rates of return to investment in education around the world", in *Comparative Education Review* (Madison, Wis.), Vol. 16, No. 1, Feb. 1972.

[3] Although once it were altered, the consequences could be assessed by means of a new rate-of-return calculation.

Table 1. Private and social rates of return by educational levels in developed and less developed countries

Countries	Secondary education		Higher education	
	Private rate	Social rate	Private rate	Social rate
Developed	11.9 (7)	9.5 (8)	11.9 (11)	9.4 (10)
Less developed	18.5 (14)	15.2 (18)	22.0 (14)	12.4 (8)

Source : Psacharopoulos, op. cit., Ch. 4.
NB : the number of country observations are in parentheses. The dividing line between countries is GNP per head of US$1,000.

carry the reallocation of resources because rates of return provide only signals of direction, not statements of actual amounts to aim at. However, the discrepancies in rates of return to the different levels of education are, in most cases, so large that even huge shifts of resources over a period of five to ten years would not suffice to close the gap.[1] It is sometimes said that, in so far as the causes of wastage in primary education are largely a matter of poverty and deprived home background, there is little the educational authorities can do to increase attendance rates in primary schools. But free meals, free uniforms and free bussing, not to mention smaller classes and better-trained teachers, can do much to increase enrolment rates, and all these measures would compete for budgetary funds with the rising outlays on secondary and higher education.

The argument in favour of shifting expenditures towards primary education is probably strengthened by introducing the question of "externalities" and it is certainly strengthened by considering non-economic objectives for education, such as equality of educational opportunity, social cohesion and political stability. Furthermore, we hope to show subsequently that the maximisation of employment, whether or not there is a conflict between employment and output, likewise leads to greater emphasis on primary education. The point is, however, that even if we take a much narrower view of the instrumental ends of education—to maximise the rate of growth of output—there is now a nice consilience between the views of economists and what I take to be the view of most educators : that primary education must be given top priority.

---

[1] For some examples of "sensitivity analysis" to show how rates of return in certain countries will change in the future, given specified changes in enrolments at various levels, see C. R. S. Dougherty : "Optimal allocation of investment in education", in Hollis B. Chenery (ed.) : *Studies in development planning* (Cambridge, Mass., Harvard University Press ; London, Oxford University Press, 1971) ; M. Selowsky : *The effect of unemployment and growth on the rate of return to education : the case of Colombia* (Cambridge, Mass., Harvard University Center for International Affairs, 1969) ; and Martin Carnoy and Hans Thias : "Educational planning with flexible wages : a Kenyan example", in *Economic Development and Cultural Change* (Chicago), Vol. 20, No. 3, Apr. 1972.

It is interesting to note that we could have arrived at this result via manpower forecasting. Most of the long-term projections of employment prospects in less developed countries do in fact predict continual surpluses of highly qualified manpower up to 1980 and even 1985.[1] Nevertheless, this rarely leads to the conclusion that there is too much secondary and higher education. The probable explanation for this apparent contradiction is that the manpower requirements approach to educational planning starts off with the assumption that lack of educated manpower is a "bottleneck" to economic growth. Primary school expansion is considered to be a political decision, a question of "social demand", and the approach concentrates on secondary and higher education as the key elements in the contribution of education to economic growth. This preoccupation with bottlenecks or shortages of highly qualified manpower virtually excludes the concept of over-expansion of any type of education. Rate-of-return analysis, on the other hand, does not assume *a priori* that there are shortages of middle or high level manpower, or even that formal schooling is a desirable investment compared to other public expenditure. The finding that primary education is the most socially profitable level of education in most less developed countries is genuinely surprising, as is the other finding that the social rates of return on almost all levels of education compare quite favourably with alternative investments in both the public and the private sector.

A final word. It is important to realise that the case we have just made for restricting the growth of higher, and to some extent secondary, education is not based on the fact that there is educated unemployment. Rather it is based on evidence about the social yield of investment in education after adjusting earnings for the average probability of unemployment. Educated unemployment as such can be used just as easily to defend educational expansion as educational contraction. After all, the educational authorities might say, to cut down on university places would simply increase the number of unemployed high school graduates ; to cut down on high school places would simply increase the number of unemployed primary school leavers, and so on. Since the fault lies with the functioning of the labour market, we may as well expand educational facilities, thereby keeping people off the labour market as long as possible. The fallacy in this argument is simply neglect of the resources used in producing more educated people, which is automatically taken into account when calculating rates of return.[2] Besides, the trouble with educational expan-

---

[1] See Turnham, op. cit., pp. 119-120 ; see also Blaug, Layard and Woodhall, op. cit., pp. 243-244 ; Blaug, "Educated unemployment in Asia", op. cit.

[2] As the Ceylon report puts it : "University education is a very expensive way of keeping a handful of young people off the labour market ; the financial savings, though not large, should create at least an equivalent number of employment opportunities" (p. 144, note 1).

sion as a method of mopping up labour, as distinct from the expansion of some other equally labour-intensive industry, is that the output of education is necessarily more educated people. Thus, educational expansion does not simply postpone the problem ; it postpones it only to magnify it in the future.

THE VOCATIONAL SCHOOL FALLACY

Some years ago Philip Foster set a cat among the pigeons with an article entitled "The vocational school fallacy in development planning".[1] Arguing from Ghanaian evidence, he denied that vocational training provided within formal educational institutions could ever become an effective method of accelerating economic development ; he further denied that general education and vocational training are ever substitutes for each other, the former being on the contrary a necessary foundation for the latter, and the latter being generally more efficiently provided on the job rather than inside schools. He conceded, however, that there was an argument for "special vocational institutes being created in particular cases where their endeavours can be closely meshed with on-the-job training and with the actual manpower requirements indicated by the market for skills". Since then a good deal of evidence has been forthcoming from other countries that threatens even this slender foundation for a vocational school strategy in educational planning.[2] This evidence is rarely of the rate-of-return kind. We have data on rates of return to vocational as against academic secondary schools for only three countries, and the findings are ambiguous.[3] Rather, the evidence refers to the job prospects of vocational school graduates and to the use which they eventually make of their training.

The problem, it seems to me, is essentially one of the degree of inaccuracy that inheres in the art of manpower forecasting. If we could more or less accurately forecast the demand for precisely specified skills, there would indeed be a case grounded in economies-of-scale for training people on a full-time basis inside schools to acquire these skills. But even the most enthusiastic manpower forecasters agree that long-term and even medium-term manpower forecasts cannot be expected to do more than to distinguish the needs for people

---

[1] In C. Arnold Anderson and Mary Jean Bowman (eds.) : *Education and economic development* (Chicago, Aldine Publishing Co. ; London, Frank Cass, 1966) ; reprinted in M. Blaug (ed.) : *Economics of education 1* (London, Penguin Books, 1968). For a fuller treatment, see Philip Foster : *Education and social change in Ghana* (London, Routledge & Kegan Paul, 1965).

[2] See Eugene Staley : *Planning occupational education and training for development* (New York, Praeger, 1971).

[3] See Psacharopoulos, *The economic returns to education...*, op. cit., Ch. 4 ; Colombia and Thailand show lower rates for vocational secondary schooling but the Philippines shows higher rates for academic secondary education.

with general academic education from the needs for those with scientific and technical preparation. Since formal educational institutions, either at the secondary or at the tertiary level, invariably commit themselves to two- to three-year cycles, the inability of manpower forecasters to make accurate, detailed predictions of skill requirements over such time horizons would seem to be fatal to a vocational school strategy.

Let us be clear that this is a different, and I think deeper, argument against vocational schooling from what we usually hear. Everyones agrees that vocational schools are expensive ; that vocational school teachers ought to be well trained teachers as well as having industrial experience, but that such people are scarce in any country ; that the equipment of vocational schools is liable to be either outmoded or so advanced as to have little relevance to the country in question ; that it is virtually impossible to simulate the actual rhythm and discipline of factory work in the classroom ; and that most students regard vocational schools as second-best opportunities and hence are reluctant to take their training seriously. Nevertheless, if vocational schooling made good sense, these would merely constitute surmountable difficulties. Unfortunately, vocational training in formal educational institutions makes little sense on either educational or on economic grounds. It is impossible to foresee accurately the requirements for *specific* skills in an economy two to three years hence; for that reason, vocational training on a full-time basis must necessarily impart general skills, at which point it ceases to be "vocational" in the sense in which that term is usually understood. And on strictly educational grounds, vocational schooling frequently creates a sense of second-class citizenship among both teachers and taught which militates against effective learning.

We are not denying the case for accelerated training courses provided on a part-time basis after working hours, or even on a full-time basis for several months in the year in a rural out-of-school context. Nor are we denying the case for "vocationalising" secondary school curricula, if what is meant thereby is the provision of some work-oriented shop courses, combined with take-home projects of a practical kind (we shall return to this question in Chapter 4). But to ask schools to prepare students to take up clearly defined occupations is to ask them to do what is literally impossible. The most that schools can do is to provide a broad technical foundation for on-the-job acquisition of specific skills.

But surely teacher training itself is full-time vocational training provided in formal institutions ? And what about medical education ? Both of these, however, involve systematic on-the-job training after a period of formal instruction. No one imagines for a moment that the skill of a teacher or of a doctor can be adequately imparted without work experience, and indeed in each case teacher practice and hospital internship is regarded as a critical element in the total learning process. What is true of teaching and medicine is just as true of other vocations.

One of the practical lessons of the economics of education, therefore, is that "academic education" is not the *bête noire* that so many manpower planners make it out to be. Once again, we find that economists and educators can agree and do on the question of vocational schooling.

PRIVATE AND SOCIAL COSTS OF EDUCATION

Perhaps the chief merit of rate-of-return analysis of educational investment is to have dramatically emphasised the enormous gap that prevails in almost all countries between the private and the social costs of education. Private rates of return to education everywhere exceed social rates of return despite the fact that the private rate takes account only of personal earnings after the deduction of income tax, whereas the social rate is calculated on earnings before deducting income tax. The reason for this is simply that the total resource costs of education everywhere exceed the costs that students and parents must bear themselves. It is a striking and still unappreciated fact that the abolition of tuition fees does not suffice to make education free to students : in almost all cases, indirect costs in the form of earnings forgone while studying constitute a larger proportion of the total costs imposed on students and parents than do direct costs in the form of fees, books and travel. Furthermore, indirect costs are nowhere comprehensively subsidised by the State. Since the opportunities for gainful employment increase rapidly after the age of 12 in most less developed countries, the failure to compensate parents for the forgone earnings of their children at school constitutes an effective bias against participation in secondary and higher education for the poorer classes of the community.

As if this were not bad enough, we even get cases, as in most of Tropical Africa, where fees for primary education are fairly common but fees for higher education are extremely rare. Given the other built-in educational biases against children from poor families, it is hardly surprising therefore that, as we mount the educational ladder, the survivors are drawn increasingly from well-to-do families. In the light of these considerations, excessive investment in higher education in less developed countries takes on a new significance : a glance at table 2 will show that the less developed the country, the more expensive is higher relative to primary education. Quite apart from the traditional objective of maximising the rate of economic growth, the policy of allowing higher education to grow at its own natural rate is steadily undermining the goal of equality of educational opportunity in less developed countries. In short, far from these two goals being necessarily in conflict, I believe there is now evidence to show that both economic and social objectives would be served by redirecting resources in favour of the lower stages of the educational system.

Table 2. Ratios of social costs by educational levels per student per year (primary = 1)

Degree of development	Secondary/primary	Higher/primary
Developed (New Zealand, United Kingdom, United States)	6.6	17.6
Intermediate (Chile, Colombia, Israel, Mexico)	6.6	20.9
Less developed (Ghana, India, Kenya, Rep. of Korea, Nigeria, Uganda)	11.9	87.9

Source: Psacharopoulos, *The economic returns to education...*, op. cit., Ch. 8.
NB: Social costs are defined as direct costs plus earnings forgone.

The brief discussion of costs is sufficient to show that this can be accomplished in a number of ways: a portion of the educational budget could be reallocated from higher or secondary to primary education, leaving the pattern of educational finance what it was before; alternatively, a larger share of the total costs could be shifted to students and parents in higher education, say, via a system of student loans coupled with a rise in fees, the sums thereby released being devoted to primary education. The money could be reallocated to bring about a change in enrolments at the various levels or it could be used to convert quantitative reductions at one level into qualitative improvements at another level: only piecemeal experiments can tell us which is the better method. The possible courses of action are much greater in number than is usually imagined and, in particular, there is absolutely no reason to exclude the costs of education as one of the policy instruments (I shall return to this question in Chapter 4).

COST-EFFECTIVENESS ANALYSIS

The tenor of these remarks suggests that rate-of-return analysis or cost-benefit analysis is in fact only a species of a much larger genus which can be used to evaluate *any* activity, however many objectives that activity aims to satisfy. I label the genus " cost-effectiveness analysis ", but some practitioners of the art prefer to describe it as " systems analysis" or "management science". Whatever it is called, the method in application to a number of alternative "projects" consists essentially of three steps: (1) specify each of the multiple objectives in such a way that they can be scaled, preferably in cardinal numbers, but possibly in ordinal numbers; (2) in terms of that scale, measure the effectiveness of all projects per unit of costs for each of the objectives; and (3) choose the "best" project by applying the planner's "preference function", that is, a set of weights or order of priorities among objectives without which it is impossible to choose among a series of conflicting cost-effectiveness ratios. This is cost-effectiveness analysis, but it is also the explicit formulation of the logic of rational decision-making. Its intimate association with programme budgeting techniques should be obvious ; PPB in fact consists of steps (1) and (2), leaving step (3) to be decided "politically".

In principle all this is no doubt unobjectionable, although in practice it may be difficult to work systematically through every step. Nevertheless, it has the great advantage not only of showing that all educational decisions involve fundamental value judgements about goals or objectives but also of showing precisely where these judgements enter in. Steps (1) and (2) are positive social science, since one does not have to like a country's objectives in order to formulate them operationally, or to quantify the degree to which its educational system effectively achieves these objectives. Step (3), on the other hand, is obviously normative social science and raises delicate questions about how one is supposed to elicit a government's "preference function" without actually imposing one's own.

Educational planning in the round must go beyond cost-benefit analysis to cost-effectiveness analysis. We know that it is difficult to give an unambiguous interpretation of the economic development goals of a nation. How much more so is this the case with social, political and even purely educational goals. The fact that one can still encounter statements in the literature that profess to advocate something called "the social demand approach" to educational planning—by which is usually meant that country A should meet a target set by country B, while country B of course is doing exactly the same with respect to country A—is proof enough that non-economic goals have hardly begun to be operationally formulated. Radically different educational policies can be justified in terms of "equality of educational opportunities", depending on whether we mean equality of access or equality of outcomes. It would be easy to multiply examples for some of the other goals and we will have occasion to elaborate on different versions of the goal of maximising employment opportunities. Suffice it to say that the concept of educational planning for economic objectives may be an untidy mess but it is a paragon of order compared to educational planning for social, political and educational objectives. Is it perhaps that sociologists, political scientists, psychologists and educationists have lacked a framework of decision-making in which their positive findings may be fitted ? If so, cost-effectiveness analysis is such a framework, which would permit social scientists other than economists to make their contribution to the subject.

CONCLUSION

It would be absurd to pretend that recent work in the economics of education adds up to an impressive list of concrete recommendations to educational planners in less developed countries. What it does provide is some general presumptions, such as those in favour of investing in primary education and opposed to investing in vocational schooling. Beyond that, it offers some suggestions resting ultimately on the inherent uncertainty of the future and the limited capacity of social scientists to reduce the level of uncertainty by accurate forecasting. Decision-making under uncertainty leads, of course, to different kinds of decisions from those of decision-making under certainty : the irreducible uncertainty of the future argues in favour of teaching general rather than specific skills ; of late rather than early specialisation ; of part-time rather than full-time education ; of expenditure on the provision of information, if necessary at the expense of facilities ; and, in general, of postponing all "lumpy" decisions as long as possible. In the final analysis, however, recent work in the economics of education warns us that educational planning must take account of the functioning of the labour market. By the test of the labour market, education appears to be valuable to individuals, even though it does not always guarantee employment. We have so far evaded the question, however, of what exactly goes on inside schools that makes schooling valuable in the simple sense that employers are willing to pay for it. To this question we now turn.

THE PUZZLING ECONOMIC VALUE OF EDUCATION

3

We begin by emphasising a remarkable fact of life : between any two groups of individuals of the same age and sex, the group with more education of whatever kind will have higher average earnings from employment than the group with less, even if the two groups are employed in the same occupational category in the same industry. Or, to put it differently : everyone tends to earn more as they grow older and acquire more work experience, but the person with more education will tend to start off at a higher salary and this differential will widen with age right up to the last years before retirement. Thus, if we draw a graph of earnings on age for each of the levels or years of schooling completed, the successive "age-earnings profiles", as they have come to be called, will lie neatly in ascending order without ever crossing each other.[1] Of course, these are mean earnings of cohorts with different levels or years of education ; we are not saying that every university graduate earns more than every high school graduate, but the central tendency is nevertheless unmistakable. It remains unmistakable even if we adjust the earnings for the incidence of educated unemployment. For example, if 10 per cent of university graduates are unemployed, we take 90 per cent of the earnings of university graduates, and so on for each level.

The universality of this positive association between education and earnings (and between age and earnings) is one of the most striking findings of modern social science. It is indeed one of the few safe generalisations that one can make about labour markets.[2] If traditional education is really as irrelevant to the needs of less developed countries as we are always being told it is, it is actually very surprising that no country has yet broken the pattern. In short, it is puzzling

---

[1] For some representative examples, see Blaug, *Introduction to the economics of education*, op. cit., pp. 24-25.

[2] The evidence for 30 countries, 10 of which are developed countries, is fully documented by Psacharopoulos, *The economic returns to education...*, op. cit.

that education everywhere appears to be regarded as something valuable that must be financially rewarded.

The question before us is therefore : why do employers pay more to better educated workers ? It seems on due reflection that there are only three competing explanations, all others being varieties thereof, namely : (1) education imparts vocationally useful skills which are in scarce supply ; (2) education disseminates definite social values, in effect recruiting children into the ruling élite of a society ; and (3) education acts as a screening device to select the most able people for the best jobs. I shall arbitrarily label (1) the "economic" explanation, (2) the "sociological" explanation and (3) the "psychological" explanation, simply because these mnemonics are easier to remember than the numbers themselves. Our problem is to decide whether these are really alternative explanations among which we must choose, or whether they are all true in their own way ; and if they are all true in their own way—as appears to be the case at first sight—whether it would make any difference if one of them were nearer the whole truth than any of the others.

THE ECONOMIC EXPLANATION

The "economic" explanation is, in a nutshell, that better educated workers earn more because they are more productive, presumably because of the knowledge they have acquired in schools. The phrase "educated workers are more productive" is one of those technical expressions masquerading in everyday language that is easily misunderstood : for economists, no words are needed to explain its meaning and for non-economists almost no words suffice.

First of all, because all factors of production participate jointly in the productive process, it is not possible to establish the proposition simply by comparing more and less educated workers even in a single factory. The contribution to final output of a particular factor like educated workers can only be assessed "at the margin", that is, by holding constant the quantity and quality of all the other factors. Thus, the phrase "educated workers are more productive" is sloppy shorthand for "education makes the marginal worker of a given age, sex, native ability and work experience more productive when he is furnished with the same quantity and quality of management, capital equipment and complement of all workers as before". To test this assertion obviously calls for a more complicated experiment than just comparing workers with different characteristics in a given plant.

Secondly, the statement that education renders people more productive immediately directs our attention to the skill requirements of jobs, the demand side in the labour market. It takes a pilot to fly a plane and an engineer to build a bridge ; what could be more natural than to assert that education, by teaching aerodynamics and mechanical engineering, allows people to fill more productive jobs and in that sense makes them more productive? What is forgotten, however, is that the term "productivity" in economics is exactly equivalent to "scarcity". Someone is highly productive if he possesses something that is extremely scarce. Scarcity is a relationship between demand and supply and is therefore by definition what Marshall used to like to call a function of "both blades of a pair of scissors". In short, if everyone were eager to take up engineering so that in consequence engineers were more plentiful than bottlewashers, the fact that it takes a knowledge of mechanical engineering to build a bridge and no knowledge whatever to be a bottlewasher would not keep the earnings of engineers above those of bottlewashers. Unless employers had an irrational preference for engineers, they would refuse to pay abundant engineers more than scarce bottlewashers.[1] Conversely, when we observe engineers earning more than bottlewashers, we cannot account for it simply in terms of the technical requirements of occupations; we must also explain why the supply of engineers is somehow less than that of bottlewashers. A good reason is that it takes a longer period of training to become an engineer. And training is costly, because either there are fees or one has to forgo earnings in order to study. Thus there are fewer engineers than bottlewashers and this has as much to do with their higher earnings as the greater demand for engineers.

Thirdly, the proposition "education makes workers more productive" is completely vacuous about the precise character of the educational experience. It is often thought that economists emphasise cognitive learning and manual skills as the essence of the economic value of schooling. But education to economists is simply a "black box": they do not profess to know what happens to anyone passing through it; all they know is that employers somehow value the experience and are willing to pay for it. Yes, but how do they know that employers value it because of the contribution that it makes to final output? What if employers engage in "conspicuous consumption" of graduates simply because graduates are nice people to have around? Because competition will force bankruptcy on employers who hire people for their own sake, just as it punishes firms that buy equipment they do not need. In other words, economists fall back in the final analysis on the assumption of perfect competition to infer unobserved differences in productivity from observed differences in earnings. If competitive pressures force business firms to minimise costs of production and to maximise profits, they will also prevent firms from paying more to certain people unless these people add more "at the margin" to final output.

Unfortunately, competition in the real world is never perfect and in any case competitive pressures do not work instantaneously. How then do we

---

[1] Everyone who has tried to hire domestic servants in highly developed countries will see the point immediately.

decide whether real world conditions approximate the model of perfect competition and particularly the model of competitive labour markets ? Not by examining the assumptions of the model, which at best can be only more or less plausible, but by checking its predictions against the observed facts. The principal prediction of a competitive model of labour markets is that excess demand (shortages) will raise relative earnings and that excess supply (unemployment) will lower them. Furthermore, the model predicts that labour of the same type will fetch the same price in any local labour market but not if that labour is employed in different occupations and under different working conditions, a qualification that is frequently overlooked. It also predicts that skills that are costly to acquire will tend to command higher earnings ; that a payroll tax will tend to discourage employment ; that a subsidy to producers will encourage employment, and so on. The simple textbook theory of competitive labour markets is silent, however, about the length of time it takes to produce a response when the market is out of equilibrium and it is even silent about the exact nature of this response. This is precisely why the theory is difficult to test and why all the evidence to date would probably fail to convince a confirmed sceptic.

This is not the place to review the evidence [1], but a fair summary of it would be to say that competitive wage theory is quite successful in predicting long-term changes in wage differentials between occupations in different economies, but that on the other hand it is extremely unsuccessful in predicting short-term changes in wage differentials either between occupations or between industries. Thus, if we are trying to explain stable, long-term phenomena in labour markets, we are apparently justified in appealing to competitive theory. But if we are looking at short-term problems, the competitive model is likely to lead us astray. Are the earnings differentials associated with additional education one of those stable phenomena that have persisted in labour markets over long periods of time ? Unfortunately, the question cannot be settled once and for all because data on age-earnings profiles is only available on a time-series basis for two or three economies.

What makes the whole problem even more difficult is that casual observation will show us that virtually every labour market is simply riddled with imperfections of all kinds. Unskilled and semi-skilled workers may belong to unions, and wage determination then becomes a matter of collective bargaining ; even if they are unorganised, they tend to be poorly informed about alternative job opportunities and unwilling to explore the market outside their own geographical area, in consequence of which different wage rates for the same

---

[1] But see my paper, "The correlation between education and earnings : what does it signify ?", in *Higher Education* , Vol. I, No. 1, Winter 1972, which also provides a more technical exposition of the contents of this chapter.

type of labour will coexist in a single locality. Labour markets for professional people are likely to be characterised by quite different imperfections. The costs of recruiting labour generally tends to be higher the more general is the skill that is being hired, simply because it is difficult to determine the possession of a general skill with a single test or even a battery of tests. In the circumstances, employers tend to resort to simple rules-of-thumb in hiring professional people, which have generally worked in the past. One plausible rule-of-thumb is to hire more educated workers for complex jobs that involve initiative and drive, and less educated workers for all other jobs ; in short, to lean heavily on educational qualifications as an index of certain personal characteristics.

This brings us to what is surely one of the principal economic functions of educational systems, namely to certify the competence of students, if only competence to pass examinations. "Skill labelling by paper qualifications", as Leibenstein[1] has called it, is a useful social invention because it reduces hiring costs in labour markets by obviating the need to test the type and degree of skill on every occasion the skill is bought. But there is obviously a great deal of history and tradition in skill labelling which is only remotely connected to current demands in the labour market. The duration of courses, for example, has in most countries remained the same for generations ; obviously, there is no reason to believe that this duration is now optimal for the particular skills that are labelled. It is also obvious that the professionalisation of certain occupations (such as medicine, dentistry, teaching, law and accountancy) invariably leads to longer courses and more technical syllabuses, effectively limiting entry to the profession by raising the minimum requirements for qualification. This acts to reduce the number of skills that are being labelled, and this in turn narrows the range of potential substitution possibilities between different skills : instead of brief training periods for public health experts and long training periods for general practitioners, there are only doctors all trained for the same length of time—all of which is to say that skill labelling in the real world is far from optimal. What started out as an effective device for reducing the costs of obtaining information about workers ends up all too frequently as a potent source of the malutilisation of labour.

On the supply side, there are still further imperfections: the patent inadequacy of vocational counselling in schools ; the weight of non-vocational factors in choosing a career ; and the virtual impossibility in many countries to borrow in order to finance one's education. In addition, there is the fact that in most countries, and particularly in less developed countries, anything from one-third to two-thirds of all manpower with secondary education or above is employed

---

1 Harvey Leibenstein: "Shortages and surpluses in education in underdeveloped countries", in Anderson and Bowman, op. cit., p. 56.

in the public sector at administered pay scales which are geared directly to paper qualifications. If the public sector adapts its rates of pay to those established in the private sector, and if it hires people at all ages, we are still justified in inferring that more pay means higher productivity, at least if the competitive model is to be believed. However, the larger the proportion of highly qualified manpower employed in the civil service, the armed forces and the educational system, the less likely it is that government salaries will be passively adapted to salaries in private industry. Once they are set free from the constraint of having to compete for labour with the private sector, the shoe is on the other foot.

There is after all no sense in asking whether more educated people in the public sector are more productive than less educated people, not so much because the government does not sell its output of services but because governments are not profit-maximisers and hence can produce any output of public services that Parliament approves. Governments may or may not utilise labour efficiently within a given national budget—that is beside the point—but the size of the budget itself lacks any economic rationale. Are accountants in the civil service paid the same as high school graduates ? Start a new tax programme and administer it by an increase in the total government budget ; in no time at all, accountants will be at a premium !

Now it is perfectly true that any tendency on the part of governments to pay more than the private sector, and thus to bid labour away from private industry, is checked in the long run by the decline of private investment and the disappearance of tax revenues ; similarly, the tendency to pay less than the private sector ultimately defeats itself in a drain of labour out of the public sector. However, these tendencies may take decades to work themselves out and in the meanwhile the higher earnings of better educated people may bear little relationship to their productivity, whatever it is.

Generally, the private sector in less developed countries does pay highly qualified manpower at rates that are higher than those prevailing in the public sector, and in that sense the productivity of labour in private industry remains a key element in determining the actual structure of salaries in these economies.[1]

---

[1] This is true even in Tropical Africa, although the contrary is often asserted. In the 1950s some African governments did pay university graduates more than they could hope to earn in the private sector, but the stickiness of public sector pay scales and the upward trend of salaries in private industry has by now reversed these differentials. It is certainly true in south-east Asia, even when the imputed values of fringe benefits are added to monetary earnings in both sectors respectively : see my *Summary of the rate of return to investment in education in Thailand* (Bangkok, The Ford Foundation, 1971) pp. 5-6. In Colombia, Kenya and Sri Lanka, however, it appears to be true of civil servants who are university graduates but not of those who have only secondary education : see Colombia report, p. 195 ; and Ch. 5 below. A study entitled *Government pay policies in Ceylon* (Geneva, ILO, 1971) found (pp. 43-68) some evidence that the course of wages in several industries had been decisively influenced by government pay awards but concluded nevertheless that the situation could not be described as "a simple process whereby pay changes of public employees are followed automatically by analogous or equivalent pay adjustments throughout the economy" (p. 65).

Nevertheless, the high proportion of qualified people employed by governments around the world must sap our confidence in the competitive model of professional labour markets.

Be that as it may, we may sum up by underlining the fact that the "economic explanation" of the higher earnings of better educated people ultimately depends for its validity on a broad, empirical judgement in favour of the competitive hypothesis. It must be, in the nature of the case, a series of judgements because we are dealing with a large number of labour markets, and statements that we can confidently make about some do not necessarily apply to others. There is a world of difference between the labour market for primary school leavers and that for university graduates, to give only one example. It may be that the relatively high cost of university graduates to employers and the relatively high mobility of graduates make professional labour markets more subject to competitive pressures than markets for unskilled labour. But if so, it must be confessed that this has yet to be clearly demonstrated.

THE SOCIOLOGICAL EXPLANATION

The "sociological" explanation comes in at least two varieties. Sociological explanation A asserts that the correlation between social class origins and education is at least as high as that between years of schooling and earnings : it maintains, to put it bluntly, that the children of the rich get more schooling than the children of the poor and that later they earn more simply because they have had more advantages in life. Educational systems aim to promote children solely on the basis of merit, but merit is judged not by an IQ test taken at an early age but by the capacity to pass examinations, which is by no means the same thing as native intelligence ; this loads all the dice in favour of children with educated parents, and educated parents are largely well-to-do. Thus, sociological explanation A holds that, far from the educational system providing an avenue of upward mobility for the poor, it effectively perpetuates the poverty of one generation down to the next generation.

What we have here is one of those notorious half-truths which could be resolved, at least in principle, by an examination of the facts. Are educational systems actually "closed" or "open" to the poor ? Obviously, the answer is that they are never entirely closed and never entirely open and that different national systems are nearer one or another of the two ends of the continuum. Since the answer is one of degree, it calls for a statistical analysis ; to be precise, for a multivariate analysis of the determinants of personal earnings.

A great deal of work of this kind has in fact been carried out, largely in the United States but also in several underdeveloped countries (Kenya, Mexico, Puerto Rico, Thailand, Republic of Viet-Nam). The broad implication of these studies is to show that education does raise earnings even if we hold constant : (1) father's occupation ; (2) father's and mother's education ; (3) IQ of the individual taken at an early age ; (4) school examination scores ; and (5) sector and occupation of subsequent employment. Indeed, except for age, it is education that is the most powerful single determinant of personal earnings from employment. On the whole, we do not go far wrong if we attribute one-half of the earnings differentials between primary school leavers and high school graduates, and two-thirds of the earnings differentials between high school and university graduates, to be pure effect of extra schooling. No doubt it pays to have well-to-do parents, but it seems to require long years of schooling to secure this advantage, and moreover children of poor parents who can some-how manage to get an education will make up most of their disadvantageous home background.

The question is certainly not settled and beyond further dispute. However, for present purposes we need only note that, even if it were settled, there is still room for quite a different "sociological" explanation of the earnings differentials attributable to education.

Sociological explanation B rests on the fact that all organisations are hierarchically arranged like a pyramid so that as we descend from the apex, the number of superiors and the degree of accountability to those higher up in the chain of command continually increases, while the number of underlings and the degree of independence from the supervision of others continually decreases. Those who stand at the top of each layer of the pyramid, and particularly those who occupy positions in the upper layers near the apex, must have the personal confidence to command others and must share a common loyalty to the organisation if the organisation is to survive at all. It is no accident that these positions are frequently filled with university graduates : people who have crossed the successive hurdles of secondary and higher education are likely to have acquired the appropriate personality traits of independence and self-reliance : they have become accustomed, as it were, to thinking of themselves as members of an intellectual élite and they are not likely to quibble at joining an élite within an organisation.

This argument looks very plausible if we confine our attention to business executives, government officials and administrators of all kinds, but at this level it is difficult to distinguish it from the "economic" explanation. Economists would no doubt assert that these people earn more because they are more productive : they continually have to assess new information and to take non-routine decisions and it is precisely their education that has equipped them for these tasks. The stumbling block in sociological explanation B is that it will not explain the facts across the board. What we must explain is not just why university graduates earn more than high school graduates but why the latter earn more than those who leave school at the age of 14 or 15, while they in turn earn more than those who start working at the age of 10 or 12.[1] If university graduates earn more because they are "leaders of men", are we expected to believe that this also applies to high school graduates and even to primary school leavers ?

A suitable extension of sociological explanation B, however, may get us round this difficulty. Primary education, besides teaching cognitive skills such as reading, writing and arithmetic, encourages such traits as punctuality, obedience, respect for authority, all of which are valuable traits to employers in unskilled and semi-skilled occupations. By the time children reach secondary education, the emphasis begins to be shifted to the formation of such values as initiative and self-reliance, and by higher education it is not docility which is prized but rather the ability to command others. Put like this, the theory is perfectly general [2] but, once again, it must be said that as such it is not strikingly different from the "economic" explanation.

THE PSYCHOLOGICAL EXPLANATION

This too seems, at first glance, to account for all the facts. Again we begin with the idea that the structure of occupations and the corresponding structure of rewards in an organisation takes on the shape of a pyramid and that the further up the pyramid we go, the greater is the degree of responsibility imposed on job incumbents. Employers are not sure that they can measure the particular bundle of attributes required to rise up the pyramid, but they have found from past experience that there is a general concordance between such abilities and educational attainments. In that sense, educational credentials act as surrogates for qualities which the employer regards as important : they predict a higher level of performance but they make no direct contribution to it. From the point of view of students, on the other hand, this characteristic of educational credentials provides an urge to obtain more education as the only way of securing a competitive advantage in the labour market : an additional paper qualification acts in effect as a "union card" for entry into the apex of the occupational pyramid.

The implications of the "psychological" explanation are devastating. Since on this argument the economic returns of education to society are merely

---

[1] But it is significant that some African and Asian evidence seems to show that unambiguously positive earnings differentials only occur when a worker has acquired four to five years of schooling ; having only one or two years of primary education seems to make little clear-cut difference to earnings prospects.

[2] For a good exposition of this version of the argument, see S. Bowles : "Unequal education and the reproduction of the social division of labor", in *Review of Radical Political Economics*, Vol. III, No. 4, Fall/Winter 1971.

those of providing a screening device for employers, and since the provision of education everywhere entails considerable social costs, it follows that the net contribution of education to national output must be negative ; that education is thus *not* a form of investment in economic growth and that to provide more education simply increases the scramble for top jobs without adding anything to productive capacity ; in short, that education is a social service, the supply of which automatically creates its own demand by virtue of the flexibility of hiring standards for jobs.

These conclusions are subject to some possible qualifications. There is some suggestive evidence from the United States that highly educated workers tend to receive more in-plant training than less educated workers. If this were found to be true elsewhere, it would allow us in some sense to combine the "economic" and the "psychological" explanations : educated labour is more productive but only because education increases the likelihood that a worker will benefit from job-related instruction, and it is this (and not education) that enhances their productivity. Moreover, schooling may encourage the tendency to self-employment, and the self-employed may be better managers when they are well educated. This consideration may have more relevance in agriculture than in industry : better educated farmers tend to adopt innovations more readily. In industry, the fact is that modernisation is invariably accompanied by the decline of self-employment. In less developed countries the self-employed constitute as much as 50 per cent of the urban labour force ; in developed countries, however, they rarely amount to more than 10 per cent.[1] It is unlikely, therefore, that self-employment represents a serious qualification to the "psychological" explanation.

We may conclude that the "psychological" explanation is indeed profoundly destructive of the investment view of education. The educational system, according to this explanation, is merely an extremely expensive selection mechanism which forces people through finer and finer sieves without adding anything to them along the way. No doubt, employers need some device for discovering skills and abilities, and no doubt it is economical to certify skills once and for all so as to avoid repeated testing every time a worker changes jobs. But surely it ought to be possible to do the job more cheaply by completely divorcing formal schooling from the certification of skills ? Why not certify skills once and for all by means of nationally administered aptitude tests at the point of first employment, regardless of how the skill was obtained ?

To pose the question is to hint at the difficulties. It would shift the cost of certification from general tax funds to employers themselves, and employers

---

[1] Furthermore, intensive investigation of the case of the Philippines has shown that self-employment and even family employment tend to grow less fast than wage employment (see Turnham, op. cit., p. 39).

would of course resist such a change. But waiving that point, what evidence do we have that there exists any set of psychological aptitude tests that could certify skills and abilities as effectively per unit of costs as an educational qualification ? It is precisely the length of a typical educational cycle leading up to a final credential that is one of its strengths : students are examined not once but repeatedly by a large number of people in the performance of a diverse set of tasks. Without pretending to deliver a final verdict on the questions, it is at least conceivable that a degree or diploma in fact provides a more sensitive test of a person's general abilities than any number of psychological aptitude and intelligence tests (we shall return to this question in Chapter 5).

Besides, the "psychological" explanation goes too far : it virtually implies that ability and drive are innate capacities that require only discovery, not development. It ignores the whole area of professional and vocational education (not to mention reading and writing) which does impart specific skills that cannot be acquired except by formal preparation. More to the point, it ignores the existence of "internal" labour markets, alongside "external" labour markets. Firms do not hire workers in the external labour market each time they fill a vacancy : instead they tend to promote or transfer from within the organisation and only hire new workers at well defined "ports of entry" which are typically located at the bottom and at the top of their occupational pyramid. They do this partly to maintain morale and partly because they have acquired much more information about the quality of their own employees than they could ever acquire about new recruits. Internal labour markets are, therefore, insulated to a considerable extent from the competitive pressures of the external labour markets and soon come to be dominated by a variety of administrative conventions regarding the allocation and pricing of labour. Perhaps as much as 75 per cent of the earnings from employment which we observe in any one year in most economies are the earnings of people who have long worked for their present employer, having been promoted internally again and again.[1]

The relevance of the concept of internal labour markets to the question before us should be obvious. When a worker is internally promoted, there is no reason whatever to rely heavily on educational credentials as an indicator of his skills, abilities and values ; this may well explain why many employers do not record the educational qualifications of all workers on their personnel record cards, a finding that has turned up repeatedly in manpower studies of individual firms. Thus, the "psychological" explanation is at best only part of the story : it may help to explain the starting salaries of educated people but it cannot explain the lifetime pattern of these salaries ; it cannot explain the

---

[1] See Peter B. Doeringer and Michael J. Piore : *Internal labor markets and manpower analysis* (Boston, D. C. Heath, 1971), an analysis of blue-collar workers in American manufacturing.

question from which we started : why do employers pay more to better educated workers at each and every age ?

A SYNTHESIS ?

It is time to draw the threads together. As we suspected all along, there is a sense in which all three explanations hold simultaneously. Employers pay highly educated people more, even when their education has taught them no specific skill, because they are more achievement-motivated, are more self-reliant, act with greater initiative in problem-solving situations, adapt themselves more easily to changing circumstances, assume supervisory responsibilities more quickly, and benefit more from work experience and in-plant training. They not only pay them more when they hire them but they go on paying them more throughout their working life. In short, they expect them to be more productive than less educated people, and the expectation is borne out : the economic value of education thus resides principally in certain social and communication skills imparted to students and only secondarily in the formation of those "technically required productive skills" advocated by manpower forecasters.[1] If, therefore, education contributes to economic growth it does so more by transforming the values and attitudes of students than by providing them with manual skills and cognitive knowledge ; education is economically valuable not because of *what* students know but because of *how* they approach the problem of knowing.

This argument applies not just to secondary or higher education. Primary schools are run by timetables, and a child who has passed through a few years of primary education has at least learned to keep an eye on the clock. As a slight acquaintance with personnel management in less developed countries will show, the economic value of a workforce that has imbibed the principles of punctuality is not negligible. If primary schools did nothing else, they would in this way contribute to the productivity of primary school leavers. But they do more than this : the classroom communicates the notion of hierarchy, it enforces respect for authority, it instils the tendency to work to standards — and sometimes it even succeeds in teaching the three Rs !

---

[1] We now see what lies behind the recent advocacy of vocational schooling by some politicians in less developed countries, namely a patently naive interpretation of the economic value of education. The willingness to take orders but also the willingness to accept responsibility for making independent decisions are no less vocationally useful skills than the ability to turn a lathe or to read a technical instruction. The notion that there is one kind of education, called general education, which has nothing to do with the world of work, and another called vocational education, which is firmly geared to the "manpower needs of a growing economy", is part-and-parcel of the rhetorical folklore that continues to impede rational educational planning around the world.

What we have called the "economic" explanation of the correlation between education and earnings is capable of encompassing all the others precisely because it is so general. But perhaps as much may be said of sociological explanation B. The "psychological" explanation, however, is in some ways an odd man out. Either the educational system is a superb discriminant of the sort of abilities that employers demand, in which case we must conclude that this is the principal economic function of education until such a time that a better screening device is invented, or it is only a crude way of selecting people that misinforms as frequently as it informs, in which case it is not clear why employers do not correct their initial hiring mistakes as they acquire more knowledge of a worker. But, of course, this assumes that employers are continually tightening up the allocation of labour, which they would only do if they were subject to competition in external labour markets. We come back full circle, therefore, to the question of competitive labour markets. The lower the pressures to compete, the weaker is the "economic" explanation and the stronger are those of the sociologist and psychologist : employers pay educated people more because of prevailing conventions and taboos, and an economy would function just as effectively if educational differentials were to disappear overnight. This is in fact the proposition that economists find hard to swallow. But swallow it they must if they deny that competition is ultimately at work in the labour market.

The economics of education is a frustrating subject, and my view of the economic value of education would make it still more frustrating. We do know how to assess psychomotor skills and cognitive knowledge but we do not know how to measure values and attitudes, at least not unambiguously. In consequence, the precise contribution of education to economic growth may well continue to elude us for years to come and, likewise, the role of education in the "employment problem" of less developed countries.

TRADITIONAL SOLUTIONS

4

Having explored the practical import of recent developments in the economics of education and having probed more deeply into the reasons that make education economically valuable, we are now prepared to put our ideas to work. In this chapter we look at some of the solutions that have been put forward for dealing with the problem of educated unemployment, as well as the problems of open unemployment, underemployment and poverty. In the next chapter we shall consider more radical proposals, some of which have turned up in the reports of the ILO comprehensive employment strategy missions.

QUANTITATIVE CONTROLS

The simplest way of dealing with educated unemployment is to restrict the expansion of education by imposing ceilings on the number of places that are provided at various stages in the process, applicants to each stage being selected by a system of nationally administered examinations. In principle, this can be done at all ages but in practice it is only likely to be feasible at points of entry into : (1) the lower secondary cycle ; (2) the upper secondary cycle ; and (3) the tertiary stage of higher education. However, a well established tradition of private secondary education in many less developed countries makes it virtually impossible to control the scale of secondary education, which leaves the universities and higher technical institutions as the only sector of the educational system that can be effectively rationed by government fiat.

It makes of course no difference whether a government first imposes quantitative controls on enrolments and then selects among the potential entrants by an examination, or whether it purports to offer a place to all those who are "qualified" and then raises the standards of the entrance examination to the point where only a fraction of the number of potential students succeed in obtaining a place. But the latter method strikes voters as "fair" because it appears to promote on grounds of merit. It is even possible to admit to higher education all those who have graduated from a high school and then to select among these by a first-year examination ; this simply postpones the decision by a year but after that it is equivalent to the method of selecting at entry. Which of these particular techniques is adopted in any country depends entirely on historical traditions.

In what sense is this a solution for the problem of educated unemployment ? It results in fewer unemployed university graduates but of course it does entail more unemployed high school graduates. Since the incidence of unemployment is everywhere lower for the products of universities than for the products of high schools (see Chapter 1), it actually tends to raise the total number of educated unemployed. However, since the costs of producing a university graduate greatly exceed those for a high school graduate (frequently by a ratio of 8 : 1—see Chapter 2), it does release resources that may be applied elsewhere in creating job opportunities. To complicate the decision further, there is the fact that university graduates who do find employment earn more than employed high school graduates, which *may* reflect their superior productivity. Clearly, there is no hope of keeping all these factors in mind at the same time without the aid of a summary statistic. This is precisely the function of the social rate of return on educational investment, which, as we have seen, suggests that most but not all less developed countries would be well advised to restrict the provision of higher education. In so doing, they would improve the structure of educated unemployment—avoiding the use of expensive resources to produce unemployable university graduates— although it is not pretended that it would by itself alleviate open unemployment and underemployment.

The policy of imposing quantitative ceilings on the number of places in higher education, either directly in terms of numbers or indirectly via admission standards, is in fact practised in a number of less developed countries. On the other hand, it is everywhere under attack as "undemocratic" and it is obvious from historical experience that the decision to abandon it soon becomes irreversible. In Thailand, for example, where there are only nine universities, all of which are owned by the State, admission into higher education has always been strictly rationed by means of a selective entrance examination, but there was also a safety-valve in the form of a part-time open-door university (Thammasat University) ; the safety-valve was eliminated in 1967, but by 1970 the pressure for admissions into higher education had to be satisfied by the creation of a new open-door institution. Similarly in India, where education is administered and financed by state governments rather than by the Central Government, the system whereby colleges are affiliated to a university makes it impossible to control either the number of places or the standards of admission ; most colleges automatically admit anyone who is a matriculate. In these circumstances, it is suicidal for a political party to demand quantitative restriction of higher education, and indeed public opinion in India is now firmly opposed to enrolment ceilings, although Indian educationists still call inconsistently for higher admission standards to colleges.

We must remember that in one or two countries the idea of enrolment ceilings in higher education is literally impossible and not just politically impracticable. In the Philippines, for example, there are only 23 state-operated colleges and universities out of some 2,000 institutions of higher education, and 92 per cent of the funds devoted to higher education are private funds.[1] There is therefore no way in which the Philippine Government could directly control the scale of higher education, even if it wanted to. This is to be sure an extreme example, but elsewhere one can only conclude that the governments that still possess the option to directly control numbers in higher education are few and far between.

SHIFTING THE COSTS TO PARENTS

However, there is more than one way to kill a goose : it may be possible gradually to raise tuition fees to cover the full costs of higher education, thus reducing the private rate of return to higher education with predictable effects on the private demand for places ; if this were accompanied by the more vigorous use of scholarship programmes for talented poor students or, better still, loans for everybody repaid out of a "graduate tax" on future incomes combined with scholarships for the very poor, it could perhaps be made politically palatable to the electorates of less developed countries.

Shifting an increasing part of the costs of higher or secondary education to parents and students would make no difference to the social rate of return on investment in education since the benefits and costs of education to society are unaffected by the way in which education is financed. If it is financed out of taxes, part of the costs are borne by single people and childless couples ; if it is financed out of fees, the costs are borne exclusively by those who consume education ; in either case, the resource costs are exactly the same and so are the social benefits. The argument for raising fees, therefore, is entirely dependent on the notion that the demand is responsive to private costs and that higher fees will lead to a reduced demand for places. Although the empirical evidence for this proposition is actually rather thin—few countries have performed the experiments that would have generated the evidence—

---

[1] Presidential Commission to Survey Philippine Education : *Education for national development : new patterns, new directions* (Makati, Rizal, 1970), p. 45.

it is certainly eminently plausible. But can a government that lacks the political will to place a ceiling on enrolments be expected to have the political will to raise tuition fees ?

The answer may well be "yes", because a move to raise fees can be hitched to the politically popular demand for equality of access to education. A survey of the social composition of students in higher education would soon demonstrate that the average university student is, to put it mildly, much better off than the average taxpayer. These figures could be publicised, and with them the true resource costs of university education as against the private costs to students and parents. In India, for example, average college fees now run at about Rs 250 per year but the total cost of producing the cheapest kind of graduate, one in the arts rather than in the sciences, is Rs 750. Every university student in India effectively displaces 88 students in primary education [1]; in a country where the drop-out rate in primary education is anywhere from 30 to 50 per cent, the publication of facts such as these could radically alter the context of the public debate about education. When we add the fact that in India half of the entrants to higher education are likely to have gained their entry qualifications in private secondary schools that charge fees up to Rs 2,000 per year, the clamour *not* to raise fees and even to lower them might be interpreted as the demand of upper-class parents to receive free of charge something that they could perfectly well pay for.

Of course, by no means all university students are rich (see sociological explanation A of the correlation between education and earnings in Chapter 3); but an increase in fees is perfectly compatible with an increase in scholarships. This is a case in which we can have our cake and eat it : we can choose *any* social composition of students we like, provided we are willing to subsidise in relation to parental income. To be sure, if we increase fees and then use all the extra revenue to finance poor students, we defeat the original purpose of bringing about a decline in enrolments. We thus face a typical problem of trading off the objective of shifting more of the costs to parents against that of equalising access to higher education, subject to the over-all constraint that the total numbers of students must decline.

What we must not do is to give scholarships *solely* on grounds of past educational performance ; the effect of that is necessarily to give more to the children of the well-to-do. We must tie the scholarship both to ability and, above all, to parental income, particularly in countries with a small tax base where the bulk of parents will turn out to be self-employed professionals who evade income tax as a matter of course. To give up because of these difficulties is to give up the goal of equality of educational opportunity, a goal

---

[1] See Chapter 2, table 2.

to which almost all the less developed countries subscribe as an article of faith. Unfortunately, the article of faith is usually satisfied by abolishing fees at the lower levels of education, leaving access to the upper levels to be determined by merit. What could be fairer ? The recognition that this sort of argument is untenable should be precisely the object of the propaganda campaign that ought to precede the drive to raise university fees.

Parental income could be assessed on the basis of father's occupation, and a scale of average incomes per occupation could then be established on the basis of the best evidence available. Parents would be presumed to earn the incomes corresponding to the scale but an appeal board could be set up to adjudicate any claims of incomes below the scale. The entire system could be administered on a regional, provincial or state level and the scholarships would be given to students, not to institutions, for reasons that are perhaps obvious. This would be a rough-and-ready method and would inevitably be unfair in some individual cases. But on the principle that social policy is made for groups and not for individuals, such a crude method of assessing the income of parents would at least suffice to establish the principle that financial assistance should go to the talented poor and not to the clever rich.

Better still would be cost-covering fees, a modest scholarship programme for the poor from the most backward areas and student loans for everyone, to be financed by a special "graduate tax" on future income if there were any income and not otherwise. If the amount of the loan were so generous as to cover all fees and all maintenance expenses, the result might well be an increased demand for higher education, which we have already ruled out as undesirable. If we raised fees and loans proportionately, however, the result would be to discourage the demand for places because the "graduate tax" would constitute a net increase in the private costs of higher education over the situation prevailing hitherto.[1] The magnitude of the loan and the corresponding graduate tax could be varied from time to time to produce whatever scale of higher education might be thought desirable. It is certain that a scheme such as this would give students a greater incentive to study and it is at least plausible that it would encourage poorer students and more women to seek higher education. It could be defended politically on grounds of the benefit principle of taxation (that graduates earn more, and that there is no reason why the average taxpayer who earns less should be asked to subsidise higher education for the fortunate few) and on grounds of equity (that it is the only system to give everyone equal access to funds and then tax them alike). It would be even

---

[1] Of course, certain negative aspects of such a tax would have to be taken into account if ever it were introduced.

more acceptable on egalitarian grounds if the graduate tax were made progressive. It is an incidental advantage that this tax would be much easier to collect than ordinary income tax : it is much more difficult to hide the facts about one's education than it is to hide the facts about one's income.

The loans proposal is by no means visionary. It works as a fully fledged system in the Scandinavian countries [1] and there is hardly a poor country in the world which does not operate a loan scheme of some sort, albeit for a very small proportion of students. The Ceylon report mentioned a loans scheme coupled with a graduate tax for "serious consideration" [2] ; it seems a pity that the idea was not followed up in any way and related to the report's proposals for qualitative reform (see Chapter 5). Again, we must add a warning that some countries face the problem of graduate unemployment even though parents bear almost all the costs of university education, the Philippines being a case in point. In the Philippines, therefore, the problem is that of making higher education more expensive by somehow inducing the private universities and colleges to raise their quality and therefore their fees. The Presidential Commission to Survey Philippine Education has adopted an accreditation scheme whereby colleges may borrow from a public loans fund if they agree to maintain certain minimum standards of educational provision ; these standards involve increased costs, and the hope is that they will increasingly raise their fees as they join the accreditation scheme. This is not the place to discuss the pros and cons of this policy, except to remark that a tax on higher educational institutions would achieve the same results more directly. Apparently, however, the notion of taxing educational institutions is considered too radical even to mention. This illustrates the difficulty of attempting to control the scale of something that enjoys a great deal of public esteem.

RURALISATION OF CURRICULA

We turn now from quantity to quality to confront the widely held belief that there is something about schooling in the less developed countries that makes students unemployable. The argument runs as follows. Since less developed countries are essentially agrarian economies, with as much as 50 to 80 per cent of the labour force engaged in agriculture, it is only natural to think that it is the failure to teach agriculture and to instil a "love for farming" in primary schools that is at the root of the problem of urban employment. Given the limited growth of job opportunities in both the organised and

---

[1] See M. Woodhall : *Student loans : a review of experience in Scandinavia and elsewhere* (London, Harrap, 1971).

[2] Ceylon report, p. 146.

unorganised sectors, it is agriculture and agriculture alone that holds out the prospects of absorbing the teeming numbers. If education promotes the tendency to leave farming, it contributes to, indeed causes, unemployment. The solution is to "ruralise" the curriculum of primary schools, that is, to infuse it throughout with references to agriculture and to introduce practical work exemplifying good farming practice. The argument is obvious and it has been passionately advocated, largely with reference to Africa, by such writers as Thomas Balogh and René Dumont. But I believe that it is wrong.

Let us begin by noting that the argument is as old as the hills.[1] In the words of the famous Conference on African Education, held in Cambridge in 1952 : "Educators in Africa [throughout the 1930s and 1940s] were constantly under criticism. They were criticised for providing too superficial an education, and for providing it to too few children; for being much too much bound by external examinations ; for being too bookish and unpractical ; for producing too many clerks and too few farmers, artisans, technicians, and reliable administrators ; and for utterly failing to stop the drift to the towns, the decay of agriculture, the break-up of tribal society, and the loosening of moral standards." [2] The item that stands out in this long bill of indictment is that of agricultural education : for over 50 years the question whether agricultural science should or should not form part of the curriculum of primary and secondary schools has been a bone of contention among African educationists.

The very first comprehensive report on education in Africa, the Phelps-Stokes report of 1922, emphasised the need for vocational rural education of the sort offered by Black schools in the American South, a point of view that was soon endorsed by the Colonial Office in London. For the next 20 years, every educational mission repeated the Phelps-Stokes recommendation, without however producing any discernible effects. Countless experiments with the teaching of agricultural science, both as an academic and as a vocational subject, had to be abandoned because such ventures ran against the grain of African opinion. English-speaking African parents wanted a curriculum as close as possible to that provided in the United Kingdom, and they resisted any modifications in the syllabus that threatened to dilute academic standards below levels acceptable to public examining bodies in England. They argued that few African teachers were properly qualified to teach an

---

1 The earliest example I have been able to find is a detailed recommendation in 1854 from a House of Lords Committee to provide schools in Ireland with gardens and to give Irish teachers and children training in agricultural techniques : see J. M. Goldstrom : *The social content of education 1808-1870* (Shannon, Irish University Press, 1972), pp. 76-77.

2 United Kingdom Colonial Office and the Nuffield Foundation : *African education : a study of educational policy and practice in British Tropical Africa* (Oxford, Oxford University Press, 1953), p. 5.

ordinary syllabus ; to add to that burden by asking them to lecture on agriculture or to operate a garden farm attached to the school was to ensure a reduction in the quality of education. By the time public examining bodies in Britain woke up to this state of affairs and expressed willingness to accept alternative syllabuses to meet African needs, the damage was done. European writers continued to deplore the craze for British-style certificates and diplomas in Africa, but in vain : certificates remained a premium for the simple reason that a taste for them was by now well established, and furthermore they were extremely scarce.

In the years after the Second World War a new attitude made its appearance. Realising the futility of advocating radical departures from traditional educational practices in Africa, educationists now demanded, not agricultural education as such, but the addition of a "rural flavour" to the curriculum of primary and secondary schools. This new approach is developed in considerable detail in the Jeffery report on West Africa [1] and the Binns report on East and Central Africa [2], which together served as the basis for discussion at the 1952 Conference on African Education.

It is [...] right and natural that, in areas which are predominantly agricultural, the schools should by what they do and the way they do it help to spread knowledge of, and respect for, the life and ways of the countryside. Most schools have recognised this and their answer has been to introduce "farming" into the timetable as the main— often the only—practical activity. Some practical work connected with the cultivation of the land, the growing of crops, and the care of stock should certainly have a place in any country school ; but it will have little effect on the minds of the pupils unless what they do outside is linked with what they do in the classroom. [...] It ought not to be possible to find English and arithmetic and history and geography and nature study and art taught in such a way that it is impossible to tell from examining the syllabus or the children's books, or from listening to the lessons, whether the school is serving an urban or a rural population. And yet this is precisely what is happening in countless schools up and down the West Coast [of Africa].[3]

The Binns report, remarking on similar conditions in East and Central Africa, stressed the importance of driving home by demonstration in the primary schools "the three outstanding lessons of contour ridging, rotation and manuring". It sketched a syllabus for middle schools (primary V to VIII) and secondary schools which it summarised as "the building of the whole school life around agriculture in the middle school and the teaching of agricultural science as an examination subject in all secondary schools, closely

---

[1] G. B. Jeffery *et al.* : "Report of the West Africa study group", in United Kingdom Colonial Office and the Nuffield Foundation, op. cit., pp. 7-57.

[2] A. L. Binns *et al.* : "Report of the East and Central Africa study group", ibid., pp. 58-141.

[3] Jeffery, op. cit., p. 21.

related to the rest of the curriculum". But even in primary I to IV, class work had to be infused with a rural bias :

> The opinion is sometimes expressed that children of primary age are too young for any work in agriculture to be either educationally possible or within their physical powers. If this were so, the outlook would not be bright, because the majority of those who go to school get nothing beyond primary education.
> In fact, reading, writing, and arithmetic can all grow out of the work in the school garden instead of out of the environment of the classroom. All kinds of objects can be labelled, and drawn, written, and talked about. Plots can be measured, seeds counted, costs used in many sums, as well as questions of weights and measures. We saw excellent vernacular readers, particularly in Kenya, and these are often related to a rural background. But what is needed in addition is reading material relating to and arising directly out of the school garden and its work.[1]

But the Binns report gave insufficient attention to the crucial difficulty of imparting a rural flavour to primary teaching : the lack of knowledge of agriculture on the part of virtually all teachers. One solution is to add an agricultural specialist to the staff of each school, but the training colleges and universities in Africa still produce very few agricultural graduates. If the curricula of primary schools are to be effectively ruralised, change must begin at the level of teacher training and not at the level of teaching in schools— which is to say that it cannot possibly reach most primary schools in Africa until 10 or 15 years from now.

This was brought out in the discussion that followed presentation of the Jeffery and Binns reports, a discussion conducted by "an almost complete cross-section of the educational world of British Africa". The participants in the Conference proceedings agreed, first of all, that to introduce agriculture as a constituent subject in the curriculum at all levels would dilute educational standards. Secondly, they approved of the idea of encouraging pupils to take an active share in the work of demonstration farms, provided there was no compulsion. They agreed that primary teaching should be infused with the rural idiom and that a general science course ought to be retained in secondary schools as a basis for later specialisation in agricultural or other applied sciences. But they emphatically denied that the schools, as they are now constituted, could unaided turn the ambitions of their pupils in the direction of farming : "little can be done in the schools until there is available an adequate number of teachers who have been trained at the various levels to teach 'rural science' or 'agricultural science'. We are convinced that the broadening of the curricula will depend, in no small degree, upon the ability of the training colleges to produce the specialist teachers of various subjects that will be required." And as for the notion that the flight to the towns might be halted by more agricultural education, they added : "We feel on the whole

---

[1] Binns, op. cit., p. 99.

that the monetary reward of farming rather than an emphasis in school curricula will determine the future of agriculture."[1]

The argument is now beginning to take on a familiar form. The Binns report seems to come dangerously close to a position which we might label as "educational myopia" : for every educational ill, there is an adjustment in the curriculum that will furnish a panacea. The Conference proceedings, however, reflect the unsentimental approach of development planners : the defects of the educational system can be repaired only in the context of the planned deployment of all of society's resources. It is the latter, and not the former, that is truly expressive of current African opinion. It is not easy to find printed evidence of this attitude because there is a persistent tendency to give lip-service to the cause of agricultural education ; but a report of the Uganda Education Commission minces no words and condemns the idea that the study and practice of agriculture in schools will teach children to value manual work and rural pursuits : "The problems of agricultural education are not primarily educational ; they are intimately bound up with the solution of economic, technical and social problems over which the Ministry of Education has no control—systems of land tenure, improved land use, finance and marketing, research and development, traditions and tribal customs, being among them all. All we can say, therefore, about agricultural education must be considered in the context of radical social and technical change in other sectors of the economy." [2]

Very few voices outside Africa have spoken in this vein.[3] The advocates of rural education in African schools ignore the fact that in a country like Ghana, Phelps-Stokes-like proposals have marked every major document relating to education in the last hundred years, yet the actual Ghanaian system of education continues to emphasise general rather than vocational education. The reason for this is simply that throughout the colonial period there was a relatively greater demand for clerical and commercial employees than for technically trained people and to a considerable extent this continues to be the case. As one author points out : "Those who criticise the 'irrational' nature of African demand for 'academic' as opposed to 'vocational' education fail to

---

[1] United Kingdom Colonial Office and the Nuffield Foundation, op. cit., p. 171 ; see also pp. 155-156.

[2] *Education in Uganda : the report of the Uganda Education Commission, 1963* (Entebbe Government Printing Office, 1963), p. 34.

[3] But see W. Arthur Lewis : "Education and economic development", in *International Social Science Journal* (Paris, Unesco), Vol. XIV, No. 4, 1962, p. 689, and two superb recent pamphlets—V. L. Griffiths : *The problems of rural education*, Fundamentals of Educational Planning, 7 (Paris, Unesco : International Institute for Educational Planning, 1968) ; and H. W. R. Hawes : *Planning the primary school curriculum in developing countries*, Fundamentals of Educational Planning, 17 (Paris, Unesco : International Institute for Educational Planning, 1972).

recognise that the strength of academic education lies precisely in the fact that it is pre-eminently a *vocational* education providing access to those occupations with the most prestige and, most important, the highest pay within the Ghanaian economy." [1]

Whatever outsiders may think, most African educationists will admit that the teaching of agriculture in schools cannot keep Africans in the countryside ; this can only be done by making the countryside a better place to live in, which means more electricity, an improved water supply, better housing, and additional health services. This is not to deny that an effort should be made to convey a few simple basic principles of good land use and better animal husbandry to children in primary schools and, generally, to apply arithmetic, science and even the use of English to topics related to agriculture. But to teach "love for farming" would require, not just a change in school curricula, but a major change in the training of teachers, which could only come about through a national campaign to promote rural progress. Again, it is one thing to dream up ideal curricula and another thing to enforce them. Experiences in many countries have shown that it is impossible to alter the school syllabus unless the change keeps touch with what parents wish their children to learn. Radical departures from the educational aspirations of parents simply founder upon a rising rate of absenteeism as parents begin to boycott the schools. We have seen some evidence of what African parents want from the schools, and there is no doubt that their antipathy towards agricultural education and even towards a rural bias in the curriculum is the explanation for the long history of failure in this field.

VOCATIONALISATION OF CURRICULA

One problem with the ruralisation of primary school curricula that we have not yet mentioned is that it would create a differentiation between rural and urban schools. Since children in towns know little about agricultural pursuits, there is clearly no case for taking them through a ruralised curriculum. And although most people in underdeveloped countries live in the countryside, some 20-40 per cent of the population do live in towns. What, then, do we do with the curriculum of urban primary schools ?

---

[1] Foster, "The vocational school fallacy", op. cit., p. 145. This theme is further developed in Foster's major work on Ghana, *Educational and social change in Ghana*, op. cit., particularly pp. 137-139 and 294-295. See also Archibald Callaway : *Educational planning and unemployed youth*, Fundamentals of Educational Planning, 14 (Paris, Unesco : International Institute for Educational Planning, 1971) ; Guy Hunter : *Manpower, employment and education in the rural economy of Tanzania*, African Research Monographs, 9 (Paris, Unesco : Institute for Educational Planning, 1966), and idem : "Employment policy in Tropical Africa : the need for radical revision", in *International Labour Review*, Vol. 105, No. 1, Jan. 1972.

A perfectly general approach to this question, which would encompass the merits of a ruralised curriculum in the countryside and deal simultaneously with the quite different problems of urban schools, is that of the concept of "work experience in schools" as proposed, for example, by the Indian Education Commission report.[1] Work experience embodied in schooling is defined by the Commission as "participation in productive work in school, in the home, in a workshop, on a farm, in a factory or in any other productive situation"—that is to say, vegetable gardening, paperwork, woodwork, metalwork, tailoring and needlework, repair of electrical appliances, spinning and weaving, and so on, i.e. manual and not mental work. They explain that such projects must be carried out inside or outside the school so as to provide students with some income from self-employment. In this way, students would "earn and learn", thereby acquiring "developmental" values and attitudes.

The Commissioners were perfectly aware of the stupendous problems involved in organising such activities for literally millions of students, not to mention the financial strain of preparing new curricula and retraining teachers to make creative use of "work experience" in formal classwork. Nevertheless, they were convinced that this approach would pay "adequate dividends in the long run".

So it will, if the long run is long enough and if the object of "work experience" is either to earn or to learn. But what if it tries to do both ? There are many work projects that will allow children to make money, and undeniably the experience of earning money encourages a sense of self-reliance—that is, it fosters "developmental" values. It is also true, however, that most of the money-making activities that children can take up have little intrinsic interest ; whatever they learn from it is learned in a few days. On the other hand, the sort of projects that teach much (combing raw cotton, dyeing it, spinning it by hand and weaving it on hand looms) tend to be unremunerative because they cannot be adapted to local demand and marketed at competitive prices. The attempt to find projects that are both educationally instructive and economically remunerative for several hundred children in a single school creates impossible demands on the teachers, even if they are assisted by administrators specially appointed for the purpose. In short, we must have serious reservations about the whole idea of "work experience in schools", at least as it is presented in the Education Commission report.[2]

---

[1] Government of India, Ministry of Education : *Education and national development : report of the Education Commission 1964-66* (Delhi, 1966), pp. 7-8, 348 et seq.

[2] The state of Maharashtra in India has been carrying out a pilot project in the concept of "work experience". The results of this experiment are not yet to hand, but I would expect them to show, when they are made available, that it is in fact impossible to combine earning and learning in schools.

We can rescue the idea, however, if we drop the notion of money-making "work experience". We are then left with what in America are simply called "shop courses" or "practical projects", in which students get their hands dirty as an integral part of primary and secondary schooling. But this is simply good educational practice that would enliven the dreary, oral tradition of teaching that is all too common in less developed countries. It is difficult to believe, however, that it would have a noticeable effect on the "employment problem". Students will emerge from the school system having learned a variety of crafts, some of which have proved lucrative while studying, and it is conceivable that this will affect their job aspirations; it is even conceivable that it will encourage them to make their own way rather than to seek wage employment. But it is far from certain that it will have these desirable effects (we shall take up this theme in a moment).

In short, we must not think of the work experience idea as providing a remedy, particularly in the short run, for either educated unemployment, open unemployment, or poverty. There are many good arguments for the "vocationalisation" of curricula—I would prefer to say a practical bias— but employment creation is not one of them. Above all, in my view we must abandon any notion that vocationalisation can prepare students for specific occupations, notwithstanding the fact that this appears to be just what the Education Commission report had in mind in proposing to create special sections in the education departments of individual states, which would conti- nuously monitor the "manpower requirements of local areas" as a guide to the work experience activities of local schools. But since such forecasts could at least provide information two or three years hence, it is difficult to see just how the monitoring services would be related to the work experience programmes of individual schools. To tie the two closely together is to run the danger of falling into what Foster called "the vocational school fallacy" (see Chapter 2). So long as pupils are in fact earning income from "work experience", it is unlikely that work experience will become frozen around a set of ossified crafts. And if they are not, it hardly matters. The idea of tying the work experience programme to detailed manpower forecasts is bound to lead to disappointments when the students enter the labour market, where in all probability they will make little *specific* use of the skills acquired while studying. Let us recall our earlier contention that the vocational function of education resides largely in the domain of value training and not in the domain of cogni- tive knowledge.

TRAINING FOR SELF-EMPLOYMENT

We argued in Chapter 3 that the values inculcated by schools are, roughly speaking, of two kinds: at the higher levels, children are taught to give orders;

at the lower levels, they are taught to take them. That this is a crude view of the problem is obvious the moment we remember the large number of children in less developed countries who take up self-employment : they end up running a farm or a small shop in the unorganised part of the urban economy. There are no authoritative statistics on the proportion of people who are economically engaged on their own in these countries, but a figure such as 30 to 40 per cent is probably a fair guess for Africa and Asia [1], the corresponding figure in advanced countries being almost never more than 10 per cent, a heavy share of which represents professional men such as doctors and lawyers. The self-employed neither give orders nor take them : instead they make decisions in the presence of uncertainty. If they are successful, they begin to employ others and in effect become entrepreneurs. Can the educational system encourage the desire to take up self-employment and thereby to create jobs in the literal sense of the term ? If so, it would satisfy the fondest hopes of all those who believe that education can make a direct, positive contribution to the solution of the "employment problem".

We may as well confess at the outset that we cannot give a definite answer to the question. The particular value we would like to promote is known as "achievement motivation" : a built-in desire to excel for its own sake, requiring no external pressures. The leading expert on this psychological motive is David McClelland, who has developed a test that scales this attitude and even measures its presence in past societies by means of content analysis of their literature. In his major work, *The achieving society* [2], he took the view that achievement motivation is almost exclusively produced by early upbringing and denied the idea that it could be actively fostered by schools : a child of 6 or 7 was already too old to be indoctrinated in this way. Since then he has gone on to experiment in India with intensive training courses in achievement motivation for adults who are already entrepreneurs. In a long and complex attempt to evaluate these courses, he reaches the general conclusion that they are effective in most cases but certainly not in all ; the reasons for failure with some individuals is not altogether clear. [3] This does not help us much in understanding how one might train children to be achievement-motivated, but it does highlight the pervasive lack of knowledge about the determinants of the formation

---

[1] The Kenya report estimates that 20 per cent of the labour force in Nairobi is employed in the so-called "informal sector", the figure in other Kenyan towns running as high as 50 per cent. Many of these people, however, are working for small entrepreneurs and are therefore not self-employed. Similarly, in agriculture, the bulk of youngsters work on family farms under the direction of their parents.

[2] *The achieving society* (Princeton, NJ, Van Nostrand, 1961).

[3] See David C. McClelland and David G. Winter : *Motivating economic achievement* (New York, The Free Press ; London, Collier-Macmillan, 1969). It must be said that this was an exploratory field experiment made up of only 82 individual observations with a control group of 73 individuals.

of values. Clearly, if we knew precisely how values formed, we could instil them.

It is probably true to say that self-help and achievement drive are typically instilled, not only by child-rearing practices, but by the entire culture of a society which a child soaks up without even being aware of it. It is paradoxical that while some talk of educational reform to promote self-employment in less developed countries, others in the same country extol the virtues of industrialisation through central planning. Now whatever the rights and wrongs of central planning, it is difficult to combine a belief in the omniscience and benevolence of governments with a belief in the merits of entrepreneurship. It does seem, therefore, that the climate of opinion in less developed countries today is perfectly designed to encourage wage employment in the public sector and not self-employment in the unorganised sector. If self-employment is more prevalent in less developed than in developed countries, it is surely because inadequate opportunities for wage employment drive large numbers of students to self-employment as a last resort ? The educational system can hardly be made accountable for the prevalence of self-employment, much less blamed because it is not more prevalent. Furthermore, the process of development seems to be associated with the decline of self-employment (see Chapter 1). In any case, we simply do not know how to teach children to be entrepreneurs ; once they have left school, of course, we can provide non-formal institutions that will train them to make things and to sell them, but this is hardly what is meant by "training for self-employment". There is a vast literature on entrepreneurship, but little of it implies that schools have much to do with the making of entrepreneurs.

ADULT LITERACY CAMPAIGNS

If school education can make people more productive, so can literacy campaigns. If school education can promote "developmental" values, so can literacy campaigns. If school education can stimulate entrepreneurship, so can literacy campaigns. There is little we can say about the effects of education on children that does not also apply to literacy campaigns for adults. Moreover, the costs are invariably less and the benefits come much sooner. Why then is adult literacy so neglected, rarely accounting for more than 3 to 5 per cent of educational budgets in less developed countries ?

First of all, there is genuine doubt that the benefits of adult literacy campaigns approach those of school education. Firstly, and from our point of view most significantly, literacy courses are usually too short to have much effect on attitudes. Secondly, most literacy campaigns succeed in imparting only rudimentary literacy, which soon peters out without lasting effects. Thirdly, the economic demand for literate workers in less developed countries is more limited than is usually believed, in consequence of which literacy campaigns tend to cater largely for women and older people. And, fourthly, the economic benefits of literacy make themselves felt not so much directly in terms of the literate adult as indirectly via, say, the enhanced productivity of agricultural extension officers.

Recognising these defects of mass literacy campaigns, Unesco launched the World Experimental Literacy Programme in 1963, which is now drawing to a close in eight countries. The watchword of the Unesco programme was "the selective, intensive approach to functional literacy" : it was selective because it was confined to young adults aged between 15 and 29 ; it was intensive because the courses were conducted every evening over a period of two years ; and it was functional because the teaching of reading and writing was to be succeeded by vocational instruction, which would put the new skills to use. Care was taken to locate the literacy projects in areas with a demonstrated potential for economic development on the notion that illiteracy was best viewed as a bottleneck to economic growth.

The programme was launched as an experiment in eight countries and its extension around the world was made dependent on the results of the evaluation which had been built into each experiment. Most of these evaluations have not yet been published but an interim report from one country (Iran) suggests that even carefully designed experiments quickly acquire all the familiar features of mass campaigns, attracting women and children rather than men, for social rather than for economic motives, and in no direct relationship to productive work in farms or factories.[1] Certainly, literate women will encourage their own children to acquire schooling and in this way a literacy campaign can be justified in terms of effects on the schooling of the next generation. But effects so remote will rarely sway present action, which suffices to account for the lack of enthusiasm about adult literacy. This is not to deny for one moment all the humanistic arguments for adult literacy. It is only to say that the economic case for it looks rather thin either in terms of output or in terms of employment objectives.

Secondly, adult literacy campaigns in less developed countries lack the political popularity of school education because, as we have noted before, these are societies where more than half of the population is under the age of 20. If we are concerned about open unemployment, for example, youngsters aged 20 or less will typically account for one-third and those aged 25 or less for

---

[1] See J. Smyth and Kazam-Izadi : *A cost-effectiveness report on the work-oriented adult literacy pilot project, Iran* (Teheran, University of Teheran Institute for Social Studies and Research, 1971). See also a recent study of literacy courses in Tunisia in J. Simmons : *Towards an evaluation of literacy and adult education in a developing country* (Cambridge, Mass., Harvard University Graduate School of Education, 1972).

one-half of all the unemployed. In these circumstances, the impact of youth employment schemes will dwarf the impact of any adult literacy campaign, however widely conceived.[1] Thus, if employment is the principal item on the agenda, the question of adult literacy as such fades into insignificance, although it will have a role to play as an element in schemes designed for those who have left the educational system at an early age.

OUT-OF-SCHOOL EDUCATION

A less developed country in which as many as 50 per cent of all primary school children go on to secondary school or to some other form of further education has reason to be proud : the typical case is rather one in which 25 or 30 per cent of children do so, on top of which some 10 or 20 per cent never go to primary school at all. Whether the *rate* of unemployment declines with increasing years of education or whether it rises up to the secondary level and then declines (see Chapter 1), the fact is that the majority of unemployed youngsters in all countries are primary school leavers. The responsibility of the educational authorities in the employment problem, therefore, is more clear-cut in this area than in any other.

Unfortunately, what is variously described in the literature as out-of-school or non-formal education is everywhere administered by a variety of ministries and voluntary organisations and for that reason it is poorly documented and almost totally lacking in data. For some countries we do at least have descriptions of out-of-school institutions [2] but for many other we lack even that. The bewildering variety of provisions complicates the matter even further. Firstly, there are multipurpose institutions, such as the youth centres in Kenya, that combine pre-employment programmes designed to top up what has been learnt at primary school with functional literacy courses for those who have never been at school. Secondly, there are full-time vocational training programmes for rural youths, such as the village polytechnics in Kenya, that aim to teach young people manual skills with which they can earn a livelihood without relying on family farming ; in short, here we have an example of "education for self-employment". Thirdly, there are part-time vocational courses for urban youths, usually provided by the Ministry of Labour. Fourthly, there are correspondence courses in technical subjects, usually provided by private enterprise, which are inextricably confused with cramming schools whose aim it is to help youngsters to acquire the qualifications to re-enter the formal educational system. Fifthly, there is technical

---

[1] Many youth schemes, however, will contain literacy components.

[2] See, in particular, J. R. Sheffield and V. P. Diejomaoh : *Non-formal education in African development* (New York, African-American Institute, 1972).

training provided by the military and the police. Sixthly, there is a vast network of apprenticeship training schemes which in the unorganised sector is reminiscent of the guilds system of the Middle Ages. Seventhly, there are youth clubs which, in addition to social objectives, may also aim to provide vocational training : young farmers' clubs in many countries are a good example. Lastly, there are national youth service programmes, such as the Agricultural Development Corps in Sri Lanka, the Indian Labour and Social Service Camps, and the Iranian Army Literacy Corps, which consists of work projects in rural areas combined with training, sometimes but not always involving military service.

So great is the diversity of these schemes that any typology can only describe them crudely. They appear to serve either as a second chance of obtaining formal schooling for those who missed it earlier, or as an extension of formal schooling to help individuals to take up specific occupations, or finally as a means of upgrading the skills of those already employed. They differ radically in different countries in terms of the age and education of the clientele, in terms of the length of training provided or the period of service required, in terms of the methods and style of training and in the degree to which they are focused on benefits to the individual or on service to the community. In consequence, it is virtually impossible to assess their effectiveness, particularly as many of them were hastily set up in emergency conditions without prior planning. However, it is almost certain that in many countries these schemes cater for a larger number of people than do schools at the secondary and tertiary levels. We reach the uncomfortable conclusion, therefore, that perhaps the major impact of the educational system on the employment problem is to prepare children more or less adequately to benefit from subsequent out-of-school education—and to pre-empt funds that might otherwise have gone towards non-formal provision for youngsters. Educated unemployment of high school and university graduates may be the most dramatic aspect of the "employment problem" of less developed countries, but numerically it is trivial compared to the magnitude of the "school leaver problem". A detailed accounting and then a careful assessment of out-of-school provision is therefore one of the principal desiderata in the World Employment Programme.[1]

It is my hunch, although I know of no systematic evidence to support it, that the economic value of out-of-school education vastly exceeds that of formal schooling. For one thing, students in out-of-school education are

---

[1] See ILO : *Scope, approach and content of research-oriented activities of the World Employment Programme*, op. cit., pp. 69-85. Sheffield and Diejomaoh, op. cit., incorporated cost-benefit data wherever such data was available for each of the 80-odd institutions they looked at. In fact, very little emerged apart from some comparative cost figures.

better motivated. For another, out-of-school education is better linked to local needs and is more responsive to community pressures. But above all, out-of-school institutions have the flexibility that formal schooling lacks : there is no pretention that the past is a good guide to the future and, above all, there is no tacit assumption that what is being done is so obviously meritorious that evaluation is unnecessary. In this area there is hope that experiments will be made and that new methods and new institutions will be extended only if they are found to be effective.

RADICAL SOLUTIONS

5

We now broach more radical lines of attack on the "employment problem", running all the way from wage controls to recurrent education to the deschooling of society. We begin with direct intervention in the labour market, which admittedly is not something that ministries of education can contemplate by themselves. However, so direct is the impact on the educational system of certain kinds of intervention in labour markets that any action would necessarily involve the educational authorities. In discussing this question, therefore, we depart little from our terms of reference.

INTERVENTION IN THE LABOUR MARKET

Suppose one accepts the thesis that, say, in India there is now overinvestment in higher education. For present purposes, it hardly matters whether one has come to that view via rate-of-return analysis [1] or via the manpower forecasting approach [2], as both agree that higher education in India should somehow be cut back. The puzzling question that then arises is : in the face of rates of educated unemployment of 10 to 15 per cent, why do students persist in demanding higher education ? It is too easy to dismiss this demand as merely a search for status and prestige in a society that places an irrational value on paper qualifications. Actually, secondary and higher education in India still pay off handsomely to Indian students in terms of future earnings, even after allowing for the private costs of education and the possibility of being unem-

---

[1] As in Blaug, Layard and Woodhall, op. cit.

[2] The Indian Education Commission report, leaning heavily on the manpower requirements approach, did reach the conclusion that the rate of growth of higher education in India should be reduced over the next two decades. However, their case for primary education was made on entirely different grounds.

ployed for a considerable period of time.[1] In that sense, the notion of prestige from having received higher education explains little, because in all societies prestige generally accrues to those with higher incomes. No doubt, part of the answer lies in the difference between the social and the private costs of education ; heavy subsidies to education can lead to favourable private signals despite unfavourable social signals. But it is unlikely that this is the whole answer because less developed countries like the Philippines manage to combine graduate unemployment with virtually no subsidies to higher education (see Chapter 4). The mystery is adequately resolved only by considering the operation of labour markets in less developed countries.

Economic theory predicts falling wage rates in the presence of unemployment. And indeed, educated unemployment in a country like India has led to a steady decline in the real earnings associated with educational qualifications. That is to say, there has been widespread and continuous upgrading of minimum hiring standards in Indian labour markets ever since independence in 1947 : jobs that used to be filled by matriculates (such as clerks, typists, bus conductors and railway ticket agents) now typically call for graduate qualifications and sometimes for even two or three degrees. In that sense, unemployment among the Indians has in fact led to a reduction in their relative earnings over a 25-year period, exactly as predicted by economic textbooks.[2] Nevertheless, earnings have never declined fast enough to erode the financial incentive to acquire still more education. That is to say, Indian labour markets do respond to unemployment but only sluggishly and with very long time lags, and in this lies the key to the problem of educated unemployment in India.

The factors that reduce the response rate in Indian labour markets are to be found on both the side of demand and on the side of supply. On the demand side, there are strong taboos in Indian industry about changing jobs, and this alone makes it perfectly rational for a new entrant into the labour market to spend a long time finding the best possible job available ; but if the same number of people in a labour market spend six instead of three months searching for a job, the rate of unemployment that we will observe at any moment in time will be twice as high. Similarly, on the supply side, Indian jobseekers rely to an almost unimaginable degree on personal contacts as the principal source of job offers, which again tends to lengthen the period of search ; furthermore, the institution of the "joint family" reduces the incentive of jobseekers to cut down on the length of search, since an unemployed Indian student

---

[1] Likewise, the Ceylon report observes : "Even after allowing for the risks of unemployment, education in Ceylon is still richly rewarding for those who reach the higher levels" (p. 120 ; see also pp. 21, 31-33).

[2] There is similar but less clear-cut evidence for Ceylon over the years 1953-70 : see Ceylon report, table 22, p. 120.

can rely almost indefinitely on some financial support from his family. All of which can be summed up by saying that the persistence of educated unemployment in India ever since independence is essentially explained by certain characteristic institutional features of Indian labour markets that slow down the rate at which the unemployed are willing to lower their "reservation price", or, to put it baldly, to take a job at any price.

Thus, the Ceylon and Kenya reports are quite right when they assert that the problem of educated unemployment in less developed countries is not so much one of too much education but rather of a "mismatch between employment opportunities and job expectations" (see Chapter 1). As the Ceylon report observes, in relation to a 70 per cent unemployment rate among 15-24-year-old secondary school leavers with "O" level passes : "some of those who say they are seeking work are in fact looking only for *certain types of work, or jobs with certain minimum incomes*".[1] Now in one sense it is a truism to say that unemployment is always due to an unwillingness on the part of the unemployed to accept a wage cut : all of the millions unemployed during the economic crisis of the 1930s could have found some kind of work if only they had been willing to accept starvation wages, possibly below the biological minimum-of-existence wage. But when the argument is confined to a particular category of well-paid labour, in this case secondary-educated people in Sri Lanka who normally earn ten times the rate at the poverty line, it is by no means a truism. And there is plenty of evidence in these countries of some willingness to lower aspirations in order to find gainful employment. For example, the poverty line in Sri Lanka is about Rs 200 per month per household, or about Rs 50 per month for an individual without dependants ; university graduates, on the other hand, typically earn about Rs 500-600 per month. In an attitudinal survey of university students in Sri Lanka, most of the arts students expressed a willingness to consider jobs at Rs 300, and a government graduate training scheme which offered 5,000 jobs at Rs 200, rising in two years to Rs 400, led to applications from an estimated 50 per cent of men arts graduates (and 60 per cent of women) in the eligible years.[2] Clearly, such graduates are willing to lower their aspirations.[3] On the other hand, if they were willing to do so instantaneously and without limit, there would be no educated unemployment in Sri Lanka ; any economy, however poor, can absorb its population into active work at near-zero wages ! If they do so reluctantly and only after a long period of search for a first job, it is because

---

[1] Ceylon report, p. 4 ; see also pp. 20, 25.

[2] Ceylon report, p. 175 ; see also pp. 52 and 148 of the technical papers constituting the second volume of the Ceylon report.

[3] For other evidence which is less clear-cut, see Turnham, op. cit., pp. 54, 136-137.

family support [1] and generous food subsidies [2] render waiting painless, or at any rate much less painful than it would be in many industrialised countries.

It is obvious, therefore, that no educational policy to affect the scale of secondary or higher education has much hope of being enforced unless at the same time we alter the structure of monetary incentives in labour markets. It would be better to say "the private rate of return" because that reminds us that the incentive to acquire education is a function of both the private costs of education and the earnings associated with successive educational qualifications. We have already discussed the question of costs, however (see Chapter 4), and the issue before us is whether anything can be done about the structure of earnings.

In fact, the governments of most less developed countries are both principal suppliers and principal buyers of educated people. It does seem therefore that it would be perfectly feasible to affect the structure of wages and salaries by altering government pay and recruitment policies. Furthermore, judging by the rate of growth of public employment in most poor countries, it appears that the public sector is in the habit of "hoarding" educated people, which is equivalent to saying that it pays them more than their true scarcity price. [3] Thus, there is at least a presumption that a policy of narrowing pay differentials between more and less educated people and between skilled and semi-skilled workers in the public sector is both practical and advisable. Its consequence would be to reduce the private rate of return on higher education, thus discouraging the demand for it.

Both the Ceylon and the Kenya reports place considerable emphasis on government policy to reduce earnings differentials in labour markets. [4] In both countries, there is no simple difference between the pay structures of the private and public sectors but government does pay more to highly educated people ; what is worse, starting salaries in the public sector in both countries are rigidly tied to educational qualifications, and the fringe benefits available to workers are even more generous than those offered by private industry. A study of university students in Sri Lanka showed that the great majority of them preferred public sector employment because of superior fringe benefits, greater personal freedom and greater job security. [5] The last two items highlight the

---

[1] There is evidence for Sri Lanka that many of the educated unemployed come from better-off families : Ceylon report, p. 35.

[2] Public expenditure on both free and subsidised rice in Ceylon exceeds the whole of public expenditure on both health and education : Ceylon report, p. 10, note 1.

[3] It is worth noting that this doubles the strength of the conclusion reached above on rate-of-return grounds (see Chapter 2) that there is now substantial overinvestment in higher education in most less developed countries : if the government paid educated people less, the social rate of return on investment in higher education would fall.

[4] Ceylon report, pp. 118-120 ; Kenya report, pp. 268-269.

[5] Ceylon report, p. 135 ; see also Ceylon report technical papers, p. 148.

question of promotion policies, quite apart from problems of pay and recruitment. What makes the public sector so attractive to educated people in many less developed countries is the fact that job performance is not rated and hence that internal promotion is virtually automatic. These are economies in which many people hold more than one job and government employment effectively allows individuals to engage in outside work with impunity. A sector which rewards people automatically in terms of educational qualifications at least as favourable as elsewhere, and then promotes them with age irrespective of the quality of their performance, is obviously bound to create an insatiable demand for education. When, in addition, this sector has all the social prestige that accrues to government service in countries which either label themselves "socialist" or at any rate deplore the existence of private enterprise, it is hardly surprising that school leavers and university graduates are eager to acquire additional education so as to qualify for entry into public employment.

The Kenya report attacks this problem head-on by proposing that the entry points on government pay scales for those with school certificate and higher qualifications should be reduced by 25 per cent for a five-year period ; in general, however, the Government should work towards total abolition of pay scales, the entry points to which are defined in terms of formal educational attainments.[1] Similarly, the Ceylon report recommends a scale of *maximum* wages for the National Youth Service, wages being graded by age with a small spread to cater for differences in skill and responsibility but unrelated to educational qualifications.[2]

There can hardly be any doubt that the implementation of such proposals would do much to eliminate the "certificate-mindedness" apparent in so many less developed countries. The obsession with qualifications is frequently described as a mysterious peculiarity of these countries. Yet some of the causes of this obsession are self-evident—for instance, as we have just seen, the recruitment and promotion policies of the public sector. The tendency to pay people in terms of paper qualifications and to promote with seniority is of course perfectly rational in the face of ignorance about the abilities of potential employees and infinitely high costs of acquiring information about their performance once they are hired. And even in the real world where ignorance is never total and costs of information are not infinitely high, the pay policies of these governments can be partly rationalised as a series of conventions for avoiding the burden of evaluating people in the performance of ill-defined tasks.

The problem of job evaluation starts much further back : most ministries in less developed countries have not yet adopted a system of "job specifica-

---

[1] Kenya report, pp. 268-269.
[2] Ceylon report, p. 197.

tions", defining the duties together with the corresponding knowledge and skill requirements of each post. In the absence of job specifications, it is literally impossible to evaluate effective performance on the job and to pay accordingly. It is therefore fruitless to demand abolition of pay scales tied to educational qualifications unless at the same time one is prepared to put something else in its place. Essentially, what is needed is a job classification system with regular reporting by supervisors of the quality of individual civil servants and a machinery for promoting exclusively on the basis of these reports, irrespective of age, sex or educational qualifications.

The Minute of Supplementation to the Indian Education Commission Report made the interesting suggestion that Indian students should be selected for public service jobs at the age of 17 or 18 before they enter higher education ; the persons so selected (about 75 per cent of the total number of new entrants to the civil service) should be given higher education at state costs and their eventual appointment should be made conditional on the receipt of a satisfactory degree. The idea behind it is that this would kill off the demand for university education solely as an entry ticket into the civil service. The suggestion meets with all sorts of objections. For example, it would necessarily increase the costs of public recruitment : in addition to recruiting those who had succeeded in obtaining a first degree, there would also be the cost of recruiting those who eventually fail to obtain both the degree and the job. More to the point, however, is the objection that much less is known about the abilities and drives of 18-year-old youngsters who have completed secondary education only than about those who have also completed a university course. This highlights the fact that an educational qualification does impart some knowledge about a candidate : recall our earlier discussion of the "psychological" explanation (see Chapter 3). If we suppress this source of information, what in fact do we substitute for it ? Are there other ways, perhaps more objective ways, of measuring people's abilities ?

ABOLISHING EXAMINATIONS

The most radical proposal to emanate from the education chapters of the Ceylon report is that which demands that achievement tests in primary and secondary schools should be replaced at least in part by aptitude tests. The report distinguishes the three principal functions of examinations : (1) to provide a threat which forces children to learn if their natural inclinations should prove deficient ; (2) to certify degrees of competence for purpose of selecting some to acquire still more education in the next cycle ; and (3) to certify acquired knowledge and skills for employers in cases where the education in question is terminal. Examinations, as they are traditionally conceived, may perform one or two of these functions quite successfully but the same examination never performs all three functions with equal success. Unfortunately, as the same examination is typically administered to everyone, whether they are staying on in school or not, the temptation to cover the waterfront usually proves irresistible. As a result, the report finds that examinations are typically inefficient for all students.

The idea of substituting aptitude tests for achievement tests rests largely on the fact that examinations are known to be poor predictors of future educational performance ; whether they are also poor predictors of job performance is a moot point (see Chapter 3) but aptitude tests would perhaps do at least as well. It cannot be denied, however, that aptitude tests would utterly fail to provide the stick with which to discipline children into learning. And here we have the key to the tenacious hold of examinations on school systems the world over. In the words of the Ceylon report :

> A major objection is that to replace achievement tests partially by aptitude tests would be too much of a challenge to teachers. At present they are compelled neither to excite the pupils' intellectual curiosity nor to prove the relevance to daily life of what they teach. They can evoke effort simply by appeal to self-interest—"You must learn this to pass the examination, and you must pass the examination to get a job." Deprived of this external prop, and being compelled for the first time really to teach instead of being the mere instruments in a vastly complex and costly system of indirect ability testing, many teachers would certainly feel threatened by the challenge. But nobody who has seen some of the teachers in the early grades of Ceylon's primary schools (where thoughts of examinations are still relatively remote) and noted the vivacity with which they teach, and the equal vivacity of their pupils' response, can doubt that many, at least, would be capable of rising to it.[1]

Other objections to aptitude tests, which the Ceylon report does not evade, are their general tendency to devalue individual effort, their cruel implications for the children that fail and their tendency to penalise late developers.[2] But the greatest single objection is nevertheless the demand they make on teachers.

Why, after all, is there so much fact-memorising in the schools of less developed countries (and to a lesser degree in all schools everywhere) ? I would say that it is because the teachers are poorly trained. They are typically secondary school leavers (or even primary school leavers) and find it easier to recite facts than to encourage children to think. The quality of the teacher is fundamental to the improvement of education, and inferior teacher training is not something that can be quickly remedied.[3] In other words, if we are going to abolish examinations and to replace them with aptitude tests, the worst place to start is in the less developed countries.

---

1 Ceylon report, p. 139.

2 Ceylon report technical papers, pp. 156-157.

3 Without going so far as to say that there are well defined historical "stages" in educational development, C. E. Beeby (*The quality of education in developing countries* (Cambridge, Mass., Harvard University Press ; London, Oxford University Press, 1966), Ch. 4) is quite right to single out teacher training as a crucial element in the story.

But where indeed are these aptitude tests that will rate the natural ability of children ? Aptitude for what ? There are simply thousands of tests of "ability" : ability in a variety of mechanical and psychomotor skills ; intellectual facilities of all kinds, such as the capacity to perceive logical relationships, to perceive spatial and visual relationships, to write, to speak, to work with numbers, to memorise facts ; and effective aptitudes, such as concentration and persistence.[1] As soon as we begin to discriminate among these, we shall find that none of them, not even in combination, is equally suitable for predicting future educational performance and future job performance, which brings us right back to the old problem about examinations. Besides, are aptitude tests "culture-free" ? And if they are not, they simply reflect home background plus acquired abilities through schooling, so that we end up testing educational achievement indirectly instead of directly. Take the famous IQ test as an aptitude test *par excellence* ; although it is in fact relatively culture-free, it has been attacked time and time again as measuring acquired and not native ability. If the IQ test is rejected on these grounds, what other aptitude test will escape this criticism ? Besides, the correlation between examination results and an aptitude test has been found to be relatively high (about 0.75). This is hardly surprising because aptitude tests involve either the use of paper and pencil, skills also tested by school examinations, or the manipulation of objects according to definite rules, again a skill acquired or improved by formal schooling.

The Ceylon report nowhere describes the particular set of aptitude tests that children will be asked to take. There is a hint of a one-week ratio and correspondence course in an announced subject, which is to be tested at the end of the week. But this is not an aptitude test : it is simply a wholly new kind of examination which (insofar as teachers could not drill students in it) would certainly have a salutary effect on the educational process : teachers would be forced to develop the general communication skills of children and this would constitute a welcome step forward from the memorising of a body of facts.

The Kenya report does not go so far as to demand the partial replacement of examinations by aptitude tests but merely calls for greater emphasis on aptitude testing in examinations [2] —a subtle but important difference. Presumably what is meant is a move in the construction of curricula from fact-learning to concept formation. Certainly, there is enormous scope for reforming examinations, and with them the curriculum, by systematically eliminating

---

[1] See P. E. Vernon, *The structure of human abilities* (London, Methuen, 2nd ed., 1961).
[2] Kenya report, p. 243 ; see also Kenya report technical paper 25.

all examination questions that rely on remembering facts.[1] But curriculum reform is not accomplished overnight; it is not a revolutionary programme for those who like quick solutions to difficult problems. Curriculum reform is an inherently long and tedious process because both teachers and parents need to be convinced of the inefficacy of the old curriculum before they will surrender it.[2]

Educated unemployment is due to a mismatch between aspirations and opportunities; examinations designed to select candidates for further education become the terminal qualifications of the majority who fail to be selected; although they have little connection with the world of work, these terminal qualifications nevertheless raise the job aspirations of those who have them and thus bar their way to finding productive employment; and all the time the educational system is increasingly turned into a mere examination factory. What could be more obvious than to break up the system by abolishing or demoting examinations, replacing them instead by objective tests of personal attributes that cannot be acquired through schooling? Unfortunately, examinations *are* aptitude tests of a kind and there is nothing wrong with examinations that is not wrong with any single aptitude test. We can change the questions in examinations, we can change the entire character of examinations (for example, by introducing continuous assessment instead of giving a written test at a single sitting) and we can include tests of competencies not necessarily acquired in schools. But we cannot abolish examinations unless, of course, we abolish educational selection and thus leave employers to conduct their own examinations as best as they can.

The great danger in loose talk about the partial abolition of examinations is that it endangers the hope of gradually reforming the curriculum. Curriculum reform necessarily entails the reform of examinations because examinations reinforce the curriculum, or let us venture to say, the curriculum is really nothing else but the content of examinations. If this be true, to abolish examinations or to replace them with something like an IQ test would leave the curriculum floating in mid-air. It is all very well to appeal to "some of the teachers in the early grades of Ceylon's primary schools" (where thoughts of examinations are still relatively remote) and "the vivacity with which they teach", but it is doubtful whether this describes primary school teaching in most less developed countries. The worst teaching of all is to be found in the

---

[1] Go to any primary or secondary school in a less developed country; ask to see the examinations and divide all questions into those that rely on memory and those that call on powers of reasoning; the memorising questions will always constitute 80-90 per cent.

[2] There is a vast literature on curriculum reform in developing countries but the small pamphlet by Hawes, *Planning the primary school curriculum in developing countries*, op. cit., aptly conveys the interminable difficulties.

early years of primary schooling : most children have to share a single reader and the teacher himself is wholly preoccupied with getting as many children as possible to read and write ; there may be little thought of examinations but there is also little thought of teaching children to think.

None of this denies the fact that the educational-selection function of examinations tends consistently to dominate the function of certifying terminal skills, converting the curriculum of upper primary schools into a sieve for selection into secondary education and the curriculum of secondary schools into a pre-university sieve. Instead of relating education at each level to the needs of terminal students (that is, those who will leave to enter the labour market), the curriculum becomes increasingly preoccupied with the needs of those who will continue their education into the next cycle. It is this which, according to the Kenya report, is the heart of the school leaver problem.[1] The replacement of achievement by aptitude tests is only one of the remedies which the report proposes to deal with this problem. Other recommendations include the adoption of selection quotas and the postponement of entry into higher education (see below). In addition, it suggests a gradual increase in the proportion of the secondary school curriculum devoted to pre-vocational subjects, rising to a heavy vocational bias in the last two years of the secondary school cycle. Work projects are to form an integral part of the curriculum of secondary schools, somewhat reminiscent of the Indian idea of "work experience" (see Chapter 4). Finally, the report proposes to make upper secondary education "comprehensive", albeit with general, commercial, technical and agricultural streams between which students could choose.

All this is unobjectionable and indeed in the classic mould of the history of educational reform in developed countries. It is as well to remember, however, that the bias towards a non-terminal curriculum stems in essence from the same source as the bias towards examinations, namely the inability of poorly trained teachers to do much more than to imitate the education they themselves received. The Kenya report remarks at one point : "It cannot be argued too strongly that educational development should cease to be judged purely in terms of the criteria used by the education profession."[2] Precisely ! Non-educational criteria presuppose teachers who can rise to the challenge of new teaching methods, a new curriculum and a new set of standards for assessing students. Thus the attempt to modify the fact-memorising character of examinations and to diversify and partially vocationalise the curriculum of secondary schools must be linked to the improvement of teacher training and to the provision of in-service training for practised teachers : and all these in turn

---

[1] Kenya report, p. 237.
[2] Ibid., pp. 240-241.

depend for their success on changes in the incentive structure in labour markets. Nothing less than the entire package will work. But it would be vain to imagine that it could work quickly. This is a programme that can perhaps succeed in 10 or 20 years. If we want a quick impact on the "employment problem", we shall have to look for it elsewhere.

SELECTION BY QUOTAS

The Kenya report gingerly advances the idea of selecting students into upper secondary education by school quotas within each district ; thereafter, presumably, selection will take place within each school quota by aptitude tests.[1] The theory behind this proposal is that of equalising educational opportunity in a country where poor districts lead to poorly endowed schools and where, in particular, the quality of schooling in remote rural districts is distinctly inferior to that provided in districts near or within urban population centres.[2]

The notion of selection quotas is obviously radical in its implications for education as it would serve to undermine the tendency to promote students solely in terms of past educational achievement. Many countries already effectively practise a selection quota system in favour of certain underprivileged groups : India applies different standards to members of scheduled castes and moreover provides special scholarships to support lower caste students ; and America has recently been experimenting with open admissions at the college level expressly designed to encourage Black students to enter higher education. Nevertheless, the idea of social quotas thinly disguised as geographical quotas at the secondary level is new and, like many of the other of the educational recommendations of the ILO comprehensive employment strategy missions, is at variance with educational opinion. In purely educational terms, selection quotas are inefficient : they imply that strong and weak students will be mixed together, which clearly makes effective teaching more difficult. They also imply remedial teaching for some of the students who, but for selection quotas, would never have stayed on ; this further adds to the teaching burden. But so long as this is understood and tackled, the use of quotas is an extremely effective device for securing the objective of greater equality in educational access, which may perhaps also achieve greater equality of educational outcomes. But so long as the quotas are used to alter the social composition of

---

[1] Kenya report, p. 246.

[2] Elsewhere in the report there is a reference to a different kind of quota, namely one whose size is determined by "costs and national demands for skilled manpower". Since this idea is never developed, little need be said about it here ; it appears to reflect a desire to achieve control over admissions by indirect means.

students, while leaving the total number of school places as before, they are not likely to have much impact on the "employment problem". If schools aggravate unemployment, as some critics allege, by fostering unrealistic expectations of high-paying, white-collar employment, they are just as likely to do this to students from poor families as to students of rich families. To deny this proposition is to deny that schools are important in generating unrealistic expectations. The quota system as such, therefore, holds out little hope for solving the "employment problem", and so we pass on.

RECURRENT EDUCATION

Education is a subject much given to vogues, and in vogue at the moment is "recurrent education", sometimes labelled "permanent education" or "lifelong education". As a concept it is like a chameleon, its meaning changing with every advocate. According to OECD, "recurrent education is *formal*, and *preferably full-time*, education for adults who want to resume their education, interrupted earlier for a variety of reasons".[1] But Unesco takes a wider view : "The term 'lifelong education' covers a very wide field. In some cases it is applied to strictly vocational education. . . . It may also cover much the same ground as adult education. . . . But more and more frequently it is being applied to new activities and fields of research which . . . express a desire for evolving a new style of education."[2] At bottom, all definitions involve the idea of the postponement of post-compulsory formal education to a later stage of life, but it is not always made clear whether the postponement is to be made once and for all, or whether education can be spread in many small amounts over a person's entire lifetime ; whether some postponement is to be made mandatory or whether it is left entirely to the voluntary decisions of individuals ; whether full-time can be converted to part-time education even as it is being postponed ; whether we postpone a decision that would have been made earlier or whether we encourage a second chance in later life for people who would not have made the decision earlier ; and particularly whether it is to be financed privately or publicly, and if the latter, whether both direct costs and indirect costs in the form of earnings forgone are to be reimbursed by the State. Even the simple idea of post-compulsory education which is basically recurrent and not sequential is subject to a variety of interpretations, as is made clear by the following diagram of alternative models for recurrent education that are now under consideration in Sweden.[3]

---

[1] OECD, Centre for Educational Research and Innovation : *Equal educational opportunity 1* (Paris, 1971), p. 33.

[2] Unesco : "Lifelong education in a changing world", in United Nations : *Investment in human resources and manpower planning* (New York, 1971 ; Sales No. : E.71.II.E.11), p. 75.

[3] J. Bengtsson : *Recurrent education : policy and development in OECD countries : the Swedish view of recurrent education* (Paris, OECD, 1972), p. 8.

I	C	I	H	H	
II	C	I	H		
III	C	I	H	H	
IV	C	I	H		
V	C	I	H		

☐ Education
▨ Work

C: Comprehensive school
I : Intermediate school
H: Higher education

Model I is reminiscent of the British sandwich course in interposing work between the first and the final years of higher education; it goes further, however, by providing a refresher course in later life. Model II interposes a gap between secondary and higher education, but higher education is nevertheless completed in one sequence; again there is a refresher course later in life. Model III is recurrent all the way through, but periods of education are still periods of full-time education. Models IV and V make higher education part time and concurrent with employment, differing mainly in that Model V allows for a final year of full-time higher education.

The extraordinary elasticity of the concept of recurrent education (even these five models do not exhaust all the possibilities) makes analysis virtually impossible, and perhaps this is the reason that so much of the literature about it is at best inspirational and at worst vague. Here we shall limit ourselves to examining the economic costs, the economic benefits, and the problem of poverty and unemployment in less developed countries.[1]

To postpone the *cost* of an activity, everything else being the same, releases resources in the present which will be less valuable in the future; the net effect is to save resources. They will be less valuable in the future because, in a growing economy, resources are always less scarce tomorrow than they are today. On the other hand, to postpone the *benefit* of an activity, everything else being the same, results in a net loss of resources and precisely for the same reason: future benefits in a growing economy are always worth less than present benefits. Moreover, if the benefits are derived from education and training, the fact that man is mortal reduces the benefits of education incurred in later life over education taken at an early age for the simple reason that it

---

[1] The treatment that follows owes much to two unpublished papers: K. Gannicott: "Recurrent education: a preliminary cost/benefit analysis" (Paris, OECD); and V. Stoikov: "The economics of recurrent education" (Geneva, ILO).

reduces the number of years over which the benefits can be collected. Thus, the cost argument runs in favour of recurrent education but the benefit argument runs against it.

Unfortunately, the favourable cost argument is less favourable the moment we consider the difficulty of satisfying the condition of "everything-else-being-the-same". The major cost of education, both to the individual and to society, is earnings or output forgone. Obviously, older men or women earn more and can produce more than inexperienced youngsters; thus, the prima facie case against recurrent education rests as much on considerations of costs as on consideration of benefits.

Nevertheless, the knot in the case derives from the difficulty of believing that the benefits of education, whatever they are, would be absolutely the same at whatever age education was acquired. Cognitive knowledge rapidly depreciates with age, and if the economic value of education resides in what educated people know (which I doubt) there is a clear case for postponing some education until a later age, or at least a case for topping-up forgotten knowledge. Can we really compare the educational experience of young people, frequently staying on at school because they do not know what else to do, with the education of a mature adult whose interests have crystallised around some field of expertise? Besides, the uncertainty of the future and particularly the uncertainty of the technological future, which we have earlier invoked to justify late rather than early specialisation in sequential formal education, is just as applicable to the deferment of formal education as a whole. It is true that there are certain skills, such as those of mathematicians and musicians, which do seem to require early development and uninterrupted study for their full fruition. But these are special cases and most professional people would probably benefit from some discontinuities in their formal preparation. Thus, the advocates of recurrent education have a real case to make on the benefit side, which perhaps more than outweighs prima facie arguments against postponement. And since no government anywhere has ever applied the concept of recurrent education, who can prove them wrong?

Much of the zeal for recurrent education, however, has to do with equity arguments and not with economic costs and benefits. It is not at all obvious, however, that the lifelong availability of education would ensure wider participation of groups now denied education. The middle classes would, presumably, still constitute the bulk of those making use of the educational system. The equity argument looks best for women, and particularly for married women (who would certainly draw on recurrent education much more than they now do as girls in traditional education). But if they obtained their education after their children were of school-going age, we would lose the intergeneration effect of educated mothers, first of all on the birth rate and secondly on the educational achievement of their children. This strikes me personally as a strong argument against long postponement of education for women in less developed countries.

We have said nothing yet about how a system of recurrent education is to be financed. If it had to be financed privately, albeit with subsidised fees, there would be little demand for it, as indeed there is little demand nowadays for adult education. If it were to be financed by employers (say, by a payroll tax or by the imposition of "paid educational leave"), the effect on employment would certainly be adverse. The beautiful thing about the educational system as it is now conceived is that employers pay for none of it directly. If it were to be financed out of tax receipts, we would have to ask ourselves whether it would lead to a net increase in educational provision, a question on which anybody's guess is as good as mine. If we went the whole way by issuing vouchers to everyone at the age of, say, 14 or 15, entitling them to two, three or four years of formal education at any time in their lives, the effect would surely be to increase the annual educational bill after the passage of a number of years ? And this extra cost would have to be weighted in the total balance.

So much then for general principles. The concept of recurrent education appears in the Ceylon and Kenya reports in the modest proposal to postpone entry into university courses by two or three years, entry thereafter being conditional on evidence of work experience or community service ; the universities themselves would make the selection on the basis of aptitude tests, employers' reports and teachers' reports, and full credit would be given for part-time courses attended while working.[1] Postponed entry, the reports suggest, would result in cutting university attendance and, in addition, would strengthen students' motivation and improve their career choice.[2] Such a pattern clearly resembles Model II in our earlier diagram.[3]

The idea of postponed entry into higher education for a short interval of about two to three years would seem to meet with none of the objections previously advanced against lifelong recurrent education ; better put, these objections lose much of their force when postponement is for a few years and not for a decade or more. If the problem of educated unemployment really is one of a mismatch between aspirations and opportunities, this proposal would seem to be the most effective of all the strictly educational recommendations of the ILO missions. And if instead educated unemployment is a problem of too

---

[1] Ceylon report, p. 141 ; Kenya report, p. 242.

[2] Ceylon report, p. 142-143.

[3] The idea of a pre-university gap is becoming popular everywhere : the American Carnegie Commission on Higher Education in its report, *Less time more options* (1971) recommended "that all persons, after high school graduation, have two years of post-secondary education placed 'in the bank' for them to be withdrawn at any time in their lives when it best suits them".

much education, given the existing demand for educated labour (as rate-of-return analysis would suggest—see Chapter 2), it is hardly to be denied that mandatory postponement of higher education would result in a net reduction in university enrolments. Here at last we have an idea which will alleviate the "employment problem" on anybody's arguments.

DESCHOOLING

In terms of employment, the educational system is in all countries the largest single industry. Thus, to abolish schools everywhere would effectively double or triple the incidence of open unemployment in less developed countries. Therefore, it is not as a remedy to the "employment problem" that we are going to discuss "deschooling". "Deschooling" deserves discussion as the logical corollary of many other educational proposals for the "employment problem". For example, if aptitude tests are going to replace examinations, some children will be asking why they should go to school at all since aptitudes are presumably developed before schooling ever starts. Why not do away with schools so that we can consider all our notions of education afresh ? And indeed, this idea of "deschooling society" has been much discussed in the last few years.

Let us sum up the case as expounded by the originator of the idea, Ivan Illich, in his book *Deschooling society*.[1] His basic thesis is not that most schools are bad, which would hardly be a novel proposition, but that the very relationship between teachers and students in the standard setting of compulsory schooling, characterised by a predetermined syllabus and graded examinations, contaminates the entire learning process. Schools are thus like "concentration camps" which proceed on the assumption that children must be policed because they have no rights and no innate curiosity. The present character of schooling stems from the economy's need to shape consumer demand ; it always contains a "hidden curriculum" which seeks to develop in students "the habit of self-defeating consumption of services and alienating production".[2] The remedy, according to Illich, is to close down all formal schools and to replace "repressive education" by self-motivated learning voluntarily entered into by both teacher and taught. Children will learn by tapping one of four "learning webs" : (1) open access to libraries, museums, farms and factories ; (2) informal exchanges between learners of similar ages; (3) personal

---

[1] Ivan D. Illich : *Deschooling society* (New York, Harper & Row ; London, Calder & Boyars, 1971, and Penguin Books, 1973) ; see also his essay, "The deschooling of society", in B. Rusk (ed.) : *Alternatives in education* (Toronto, General Publishing Company, 1971).

[2] It is a curious feature of Illich's argument, like that of Marcuses, that the argument always goes back to consumer behaviour and never to the future role of students as "required manpower".

advertisements to attract learning partners for mutual advantage ; and (4) publication of lists of free-lance "educators-at-large" who may be consulted at will.

Who will pay for it all ? The government, we are told. But who will administer it, supervise it and guide learners through it ? What becomes of children who are simply not self-motivated to learn ? Who guarantees that the number of self-motivated learners will match the number of educators-at-large ? These questions remain unanswered. The basic premises of Illich's case are : (1) just as children learn to speak their own language without formal instruction, they learn other things in the same way ; (2) as most things are learnt outside school, while most things learnt inside school are soon forgotten, schooling is pointless ; and (3) any system of instruction based on the idea that one person's judgement should determine what another person must learn, and in which sequence, is authoritarian—and of course authoritarianism is always bad.[1]

Since 1961, when the creation of CIDOC (Center for Intercultural Documentation) in Cuernavaca, Mexico, by Illich and several of his associates marked the origin of the deschooling movement, the largely American literature on deschooling has turned into a flood.[2] Despite differences between individual authors, this literature is characterised by a concentration on adolescents just before or just after the legal school-leaving age—in other words, high school students. It is a weakness of all these books and pamphlets that they seem to be unaware of the learning problems of very young children, who may not be expected to see by themselves that there are certain efficient sequences for learning anything. Moreover, despite all the adverse remarks in the literature on the "baby-sitting" and "spirit-breaking" function of schools, there is little overt recognition of the fact that parents would be the first to resist deschooling and that the economic implications of deschooling for, say, the labour force participation rate of women would be serious. These are almost all books directed to an American audience, and few of them make any reference to the less developed world.[3] They mount up an impressive indictment of the American educational system, and some of the less romantic advocates of deschooling

---

[1] See S. Hook : "Illich's de-schooled utopia", in *Encounter* (London), Jan. 1972, for a brief but devastating critique of Illich's case.

[2] John C. Holt : *What do I do Monday* (New York, Dutton, 1970) supplies a comprehensive bibliography. Other books by this leading American deschooler are *How children learn* ; *How children fail* and *The under-achieving school*, published by Pitman in 1969, 1965 and 1970 respectively. Penguin Books (London) have recently republished six titles, all of which were first published in the United States in the 1960s : Everett Reimer : *School is dead : alternatives in education* (New York, Doubleday); Paul Goodman : *Compulsory mis-education* (New York, Horizon, 1962 ; revised ed., Vintage Books, 1964) ; Neil Postman and Charles Weingartner : *Teaching as a subversive activity* (New York, Delacorte, 1969) ; Herbert R. Kohl : *36 children* (New York, New American Library, 1967). R. and B. Gross : *Radical school reform* (New York, Simon & Schuster, 1969) ; J. Henry : *Essays on education*.

[3] See P. Foster : "Education, economy and equality", in *Interchange* (Toronto), Vol. II, No. 1, 1971, which criticises Illich and Reimer from the standpoint of educational issues in Africa and Asia.

propose partial remedies (e.g. educational vouchers, fee-paying education, private education on a profit-maximising basis) which merit serious attention.[1] It is even true to say that their emphasis on the value-indoctrination and social-screening functions of schools, rather than on the acquisition of cognitive skills, is nearer to the heart of the matter than much of the traditional man-power planning literature (see Chapter 3). Nevertheless, when they call for the total abolition of schools and begin to describe their Rousseau-inspired Utopia in which the whole of society is an open classroom, it is difficult to take the argument seriously. To translate burning aspirations into practical alternatives is never easy ; but the deschooling writers hardly make the attempt.

Nevertheless, if we want to reform the curriculum to maximise thinking in terms of concept and to minimise fact-learning, if we want to place a new emphasis on out-of-school education, and if we want to introduce a period of labour-market experience between secondary and higher education, and in general if we want to undermine the job-entitlement function of educational qualifications—all of which are ideas we have endorsed in the last two chapters—we must face the fact that these stand little chance of receiving a hearing so long as children are thought to have no personal rights, so long as teachers are regarded as having coercive powers, and so long as schools try to contain within their walls all that they believe to be educationally relevant to the children they have. In the effort to liberate oneself from these traditional assumptions, there is much to learn from the iconoclasm of the deschoolers.

---

[1] See, for example, Reimer, op. cit., pp. 130-133, 146-147.

WHAT CAN BE DONE?

6

If the "employment problem" is seen essentially as a problem of youth unemployment, much but not all of which is also educated unemployment, the educational authorities have a clear duty to devise policies that may alleviate the problem. On the other hand, if the "employment problem" is regarded as a problem of poverty of both employed and unemployed workers, it is more difficult to see just what a ministry of education could do about it in practical terms. Education may well be a kind of investment in future productive capacity, but within the foreseeable future the benefits largely accrue to those educated : the spillover effects on everybody else, the raising of general living standards as the number of educated people reaches a minimum threshold, take generations to make themselves felt. Educational policy as a device for curing poverty seems to lead to a single dictum : educate as many people as possible ! But the cure will come 20 to 30 years later ; meanwhile, the funds devoted to educational expansion pre-empt resources that might have been devoted to creating productive capacity elsewhere and, for all we know, to creating jobs now as well as more jobs later. It does seem therefore that a policy of *not* expanding education may at times be a more effective way of eradicating poverty. Thus, educational planning directed towards alleviating the "employment problem" in the widest sense of that term cannot avoid questions about the appropriate scale of the educational system. These questions loom even larger when we take a narrower view of the "employment problem". And in either case, the content and quality of education are at least as important as matters of scale.

THE QUANTITATORS VERSUS THE QUALITATORS

The literature on the role of education in the development process reveals a thinly veiled conflict between those who emphasise quantity and those who emphasise quality.[1] Both the manpower requirements approach and rate-of-return analysis are fundamentally preoccupied with quantitative decisions, treating the quality of education as a datum for their purposes.[2] Neither approach denies the importance of qualitative considerations; it is simply that qualitative reform is regarded as irrelevant unless first the right decisions are made about the respective scales of primary, secondary and higher education. Such convictions are sometimes reinforced by the view that qualitative reforms fall within the purview of a different sort of expert: the educationist. Those who emphasise the content of education, on the other hand, and they are frequently teachers, educational administrators, or in a word "educationists", are apt to dismiss the numbers game as pointless. So great is the political pressure for education that the notion of harnessing quantitative decisions to any economic rationale is rejected as naive. The professional role of educationists is respected only in the sphere of teacher training, curriculum reform and examinations; it is these qualitative questions that alone afford scope for rationality of the apolitical type. Here too there are plenty of other arguments that are used to support the emphasis on quality: a scholastic, fact-memorising, examination-based educational system of a given size has an impact on economic activity (not to mention the social and political climate) that is quite different from that of a practical, vocation-oriented, innovative educational system of exactly the same size, irrespective of the merits and defects of either system.

This conflict between what we might call the "quantitators" and the "qualitators" is thinly papered over in the ILO mission reports that we have examined. All of them without exception broadly concur with the findings of rate-of-return analysis (see Chapter 2) that higher education is overexpanded relative to primary education and that resources ought to be diverted from the higher to the lower levels of education. In the Colombia report, this conclusion derives in fact from a manpower forecast based on international comparisons, but the upshot is the same. In the Ceylon, Kenya and Iran reports, it derives from a general "feel" for the situation, although in the case of Iran and Sri Lanka it is supported by some manpower forecasting exercises. Nevertheless, none of the reports emphasises such judgements about the optimum scale of the educational pyramid; instead, all concentrate on reforms of the content of education. It is not clear whether it was thought to be politically inexpedient

---

[1] Beeby, *The quality of education in developing countries*, op. cit., Ch. 2, discusses this conflict.

[2] It could be argued that rate-of-return analysis is capable, at least in principle, of tackling qualitative decisions, whereas the manpower requirements approach is virtually precluded from considering the actual content of educational courses. Nevertheless, in practice, even rate-of-return analysis has so far had little to say about the question of quality (see Ch. 2).

to highlight the need to cut back higher education, or whether the lack of emphasis on quantitative decisions reflected a deeply held conviction that the content of education in these countries represents a more profound bottleneck to economic development than any possible misallocation of resources between levels of education. At any rate, the reforms proposed in the reports are concerned largely with what actually goes on in classrooms and with out-of-school education in all its varieties.

This is not to say that the mission reports are exclusively qualitative. A hallmark of the literature on educational reform written by educationists is the complete neglect of the labour market. If parents and students insist on an academic education leading to white-collar employment, if they refuse to accept an agricultural bias in the curriculum of rural schools, it is only because they are ill-informed—and the traditional answer of educationists to that problem is vocational counselling. Unfortunately, vocational counselling, which ought to be informed by the best possible data about labour market prospects, rarely is ; and in any case, the possibility that parents and students may be right, given the circumstances which confront them, is rarely admitted. What distinguishes the mission reports from educationist literature is that reform of the labour market is given at least as much weight as reform of the educational system. It is pointless to call for restriction of upper secondary and higher education so long as the labour market renders further education privately profitable. And it is fruitless to propose changes in pay scales without at the same time attempting to alter the hiring practices of the public sector, which profoundly influences, if it does not dominate, the hiring practices of private industry.

But the consequences of the relative neglect of quantitative considerations in the mission reports is that all the weight in altering the private returns of student investment in education is thrown on the side of earnings and none on the side of costs. Very little is said about the fee structure of education, particularly at the higher levels, or about grants, scholarships and loans related directly to parental income. This is the more surprising in the light of the emphasis on income distribution in the mission reports. Surely, the pattern of finance of education, considering that extra education typically leads to higher earnings, is not a negligible aspect of the problem of income distribution ? Again, the subject may have been avoided because it was deemed to be politically unpopular. If so, an important dimension of the role of education in the "employment problem" has been lost sight of.

The qualitative reforms recommended by the mission reports are focused, in one way or the other, on the examination syndrome : the tendency to subvert the entire educational system to the selection of students for progress up the pyramid. Instead of patiently working to reshape both curricula and examinations so as to certify the competence of students for the unpredictable world of work, rather than the perfectly predictable world of further education, they opt for aptitude tests as a method of attacking the certification function of schools. In addition, they want to interpose a long gap of work experience between secondary and higher education, while concentrating far more resources on the ample provision of out-of-school education.

I have thrown some doubts on the proposals for reforming examinations principally on the grounds that aptitude testing raises at least as many difficulties as school examinations. We can agree that it is not *what* is taught in schools that is important but rather how schooling affects children's attitudes and values. In saying this, we at least avoid the mistake of believing that all will be well if only we imparted vocational rather than academic knowledge. We agree, therefore, that the mere testing of cognitive knowledge is largely irrelevant to the economic value of education (see Chapter 3). But there is no proper substitute for examinations that will in fact measure the relevant consequences. If the aim of assessment is to test the capacity to reason, to digest information and to analyse it in terms of abstract concepts, the appropriate screening device is indistinguishable from what we think of as a really good examination. If, instead, the aim is to test attitudes, behaviour and underlying values, there are no aptitude tests that will measure these attributes unambiguously. We may want to submit children to McClelland's "*n*-achievement test" in the effort to maximise the tendency of education to foster so-called "developmental values", but no useful purpose is served by calling this an aptitude test. In short, the authors of the mission reports frequently write as if psychometrics were an uncomplicated field instead of the morass it really is.

Much more serious is the failure to come to grips with the implications of their proposals for initial teacher training, not to mention in-service training as related to the structure of teachers' salaries. The quality of teachers, the kind of people attracted to teaching and the way they are taught to teach, is at the heart of all problems of educational quality, and no reform of education is worth its salt if it does not address itself to this range of questions.

RESEARCH AND EXPERIMENTATION

At the same time, it would be foolish to pretend that we know exactly what would happen if we ruralised and vocationalised the curriculum, if we abolished examinations, if we selected students by geographical and social quotas, if we adopted the principle of "working gaps" in post-compulsory education, if we concentrated resources on non-formal rather than formal education, if we compressed earnings differentials by fiat, if we recruited civil servants in total ignorance of their paper qualifications or at any rate promoted them on merit instead of on age and educational attainments, if we raised fees to cover the total costs of instruction and geared scholarships strictly to parental income, if we replaced all grants and scholarships by loans at the stage of higher education—in short, if we adopted any and all of the proposals that have been discussed by educational reformers. It is easy to call for more research to throw light on these questions, but how shall we carry out research in the absence of evidence about the effects of these untried ideas ? To be sure, there is some evidence around the world that would be relevant, as in the case of vocationalised curricula or out-of-school programmes. But for most of these proposals there is no evidence whatsoever, because so far they have nowhere been put into practice.

It follows that experiments are needed. The educational authorities of the less developed countries must be persuaded that we still do not know how to make education "relevant" to employment opportunities and that in fact we shall never know until someone conducts controlled field experiments. Alas, pilot schemes are fraught with difficulties : to select a school or a district or a group of students for an educational experiment invites criticism either on grounds of discrimination or on grounds of special treatment ; besides, the impossibility of holding other things constant always makes it difficult to evaluate pilot schemes. Nevertheless, without experiments, educational reform necessarily turns into a hit-and-miss affair.

Evaluation implies criteria of judgement, and so long as there is no conflict between output objectives and employment objectives the appropriate criteria are rates of return to educational investment—that is, systematic comparisons of earnings per unit of costs for those who have benefited from the experiments with earnings per unit of costs for those who have not. But if the labour market fails to perform its traditional functions, output and employment objectives may well clash, and in this case rate-of-return signals will prove misleading. We must then invoke cost-effectiveness analysis as a more general technique for evaluating projects (see Chapter 2). It is perfectly feasible to select a particular project (say, the "working gap" between secondary and higher education) and to monitor a cohort of students who have passed through such a scheme, measuring : (1) their subsequent admission patterns to higher education ; (2) their performance in higher education ; and (3) their ultimate employment record for, say, the first three or four years of their working lives. We will probably get different answers from the three measures, and so must decide why we wanted the "working gap" in the first place. To reduce the pressure on higher education ? To strengthen the motivation of students once they are in universities ? To improve the match between choice of subject and choice of occupation ? Or perhaps all three ? No decision on policy is possible unless these multiple objectives are somehow scaled in order of importance. If the decision is made, the scale of priorities is there in any case but cost-effectiveness analysis can help to make it explicit. The very attempt to quantify the extent to which the scheme achieves different objectives serves to delineate the objectives themselves, and it is here that cost-effectiveness analysis makes its principal contribution to educational planning. If one thing has become clear in the course of this discussion, it is that the "employment problem" has as many dimensions as economic development itself. It is difficult to see what would solve the "employment problem" because the goal of maximising employment, or, if you like, income-earning opportunities, is imprecisely formulated : it is after all only a means to other goals, and so policies that achieve it in the short run may fail to achieve it in the long run and vice versa.

A GUIDE TO SHIBBOLETHS

We draw the argument to a close by means of a commentary on some widely held shibboleths about the role of education in the "employment problem" ; in short, a list of the platitudes that are heard in every country whenever men sit down around conference tables to discuss the problems of less developed countries.

1. Education increases the volume of employment

This is certainly true in the short run, if what is meant is that education itself is a labour-intensive industry, and it may be true in the long run, if what is meant is that education is a type of social investment because it renders people more productive. But in what way is it more productive ? By teaching children manual or mechanical skills they could not have acquired elsewhere ? True for certain specific professions, but surely not true in general ? By imparting "developmental" values and attitudes ? But can schools do this and, if so, how do they do it ? Unless we know that, we cannot be sure that more education would impart more of these appropriate values. Perhaps schools only sort out children in terms of their native drives and aptitudes, in which case there may be better and cheaper sorting machines than the educational system. In other words, the proposition is likely to be misleading unless the relevant time period is specified and unless the sense in which education is said to be "investment" is explained.

A different interpretation of this proposition depends on the idea that more educated people save more and spend less, and when they do spend they tend to consume labour-intensive goods and services. There may well be a relationship between education and individual saving ; however, it is not really inadequate saving that explains the backwardness of poor countries but rather the type of investment outlets into which the savings are transferred. As for the pattern of consumption spending, it has yet to be empirically demonstrated that its factor intensity is well defined in terms of the educational attainments of consumers.

2. Education works to eliminate poverty

Over the long run, this reduces to the first shibboleth. It may be taken in another sense, however. Education acts to reduce the birth rate, directly via the education of women and indirectly via an increase in the period for which children are dependent on their parents. And the lower the rate of population growth, the higher the level of income per head. Furthermore, education is a necessary complement to sanitation and nutrition programmes, and these work directly to eliminate the consequences of poverty. The trouble with all such arguments is that they do not lead anywhere : it is not enough to know that education is causally related to family limitation ; we need to know the magnitude of the causal effect if we are to choose between more education and other ways of restricting population growth.

Still another interpretation of the proposition before us is that education is a necessary input into certain activities for which there is an effective demand but which cannot now be produced at all ; in other words, there are manpower shortages and these shortages inhibit the growth of output. No doubt there are still examples around the world which are capable of supporting this extremely simple reason for expanding education, but they are rapidly becoming harder and harder to find. Even some of the remaining examples are spurious : if there is a shortage of plumbers that holds back the construction industry, it is usually because the scarcity of plumbers has not been allowed to raise the wages of plumbers ; or because one can become a plumber only by serving a five-year apprenticeship ; or because labour-saving plumbing equipment cannot be imported owing to foreign exchange control ; or because there really is no shortage of plumbers as such but only of good plumbers, a problem which cannot be solved simply by training more plumbers.

3. Education causes unemployment

Taken at its face value, this is clearly wrong. What is meant, however, is that there is something about education that makes people unemployable : it raises their aspirations beyond all hopes of satisfying them ; it gives them the wrong skills or the wrong attitudes. There is clearly something in this argument, but the point about aspirations is really true of the entire development process. Imagine if there were no education. Surely then the complaint would be that these countries are poor because they do not want to better themselves ? Is there an educational system anywhere that raises career expectations just so much but not a jot more than can be satisfied by prospective job opportunities ?

If the skills and attitudes now fostered by educational systems are wrong, what would be the right skills and attitudes ? Vocational skills, of course, and attitudes of self-reliance. But what is a vocational skill ? One that can be turned directly into the production of saleable output ? Surely, this is better learnt on the job ? Is it instead a foundation which expedites on-the-job learning ? If so, that is what schools aim to do. If it is too specific, it will not serve the needs of every student; and if it is general, why call it a vocational skill ? As for self-reliance, we have yet to learn how to instil it, although admittedly traditional education makes a poor job of it.

4. Education converts underemployment into open unemployment

Traditional rural societies share the work to be done among members of the family, each member working perhaps less than he would like. Education causes people to leave these traditional communities and to move into the modern urban sector where the same work will be done by fewer workers, the rest being left unemployed. In that sense, the more highly educated a poor society is, the greater the amount of open unemployment observed in it.

True, and yet too general. Education indeed stimulates the "flight from farming"—not, however, because it is bad education but because the same impetus that drives parents to send their children to school sends these same children to seek employment in towns : the awareness of greater earnings in towns and even greater opportunities for part-time employment while continuing the search for a full-time job. Besides, towns in Africa and Asia are poorly described as made up entirely of the modern sector ; the intermediate urban sector is not unaccustomed to work-sharing and it also provides ample opportunities for apprenticeship training. Furthermore, it is not just education that converts underemployment into open unemployment but the entire development process. The real problem is that education absorbs resources so that educated unemployment is a more serious economic problem than open unemployment as such ; it represents a using-up of resources that might have been devoted to creating employment opportunities.

5. Education is simply part of the scramble for a limited supply of top jobs

Employers will always prefer more highly educated people for any job whether or not the higher qualifications are in fact necessary for efficient performance. Hence, students are motivated to acquire extra education in order that they may better compete in the rat race; but their education does not make them more productive and hence has no ultimate consequences either for total output or for total employment.

We recognise this argument as the "psychological" explanation and will not re-examine it here (see Chapter 3). But it is curious to note how it contradicts proposition 3. If education by its irrelevant content renders people unemployable, how is it that employers are "conspicuous consumers" of more educated people ? Perhaps it is the government which is the irrational employer in question. Is it that education is relevant to the clerical needs of the civil service but not to the profit-maximising needs of industry ? Why then is industry reluctant to convert these badly educated workers by means of labour training ? And if it already does so, why does it prefer educated people as trainees instead of simply hiring able people as revealed by aptitude tests, whatever their educational qualifications ? But enough said. Proposition 5 is too extreme to be worth a full discussion.

6. **Public subsidies to further education always result in excess demand for education and hence in excess supply of educated manpower**

The argument is simply that as the benefits of education accrue almost exclusively to educated individuals themselves in the form of higher salaries, while the costs of education are largely borne by society as a whole, further education continues to be a privately profitable investment far beyond the point at which it has ceased to be socially profitable. Moreover, the much greater visibility of the earnings of those who are employed, as against the lack of earnings of those who are not, exaggerates the profitability of more education to private individuals and so encourages the demand for education. By implication, the remedy is to shift more of the costs of education to students and parents and to publicise the evidence on the incidence of educated unemployment.

All too true, and yet not the whole story. If the labour market worked smoothly and more or less instantly, it would long ago have adjusted to the excessive demand for education by reducing the earnings differentials between more educated and less educated people to zero. And if the labour market does not work smoothly and works only with long lags, there may be educated unemployment even though education is heavily subsidised, as witness the case of the Philippines. Thus, educated unemployment must be attacked both in terms of educational finance and in terms of labour market policies.

7. Excessive salary differentials in the interests of the
ruling élite are responsible for educated unemployment

Earnings differentials in less developed countries are excessive by international standards : in the United States a doctor earns three times the average
income per head, in India he earns 20 times as much, and so on. These differentials were frequently created at the time of the independence of the
countries concerned in an effort to attract expatriate personnel, and they
have been maintained ever since by highly educated political élites through
their control of the public sector and their influence on private firms. Obviously, this creates an insatiable demand for higher education, and we get
educated unemployment simply because at some point tax revenues prove
incapable of absorbing even more graduates into the public sector.

This argument is clearly modelled on the former British colonies of Tropical
Africa, but if suitably amended it has some relevance to Asia as well. It depends
critically on what is meant by excessive salary differentials. International
comparisons prove nothing except that, as economic theory predicts, a scarcer
factor will always receive a relatively higher price : after all, educated people
are scarcer in India than in the United States. Nevertheless, there is a clear
sense in which earnings differentials associated with education are excessive
in less developed countries ; the fact that there is educated unemployment
is enough to tell us that there are more educated people looking for work at
going wage rates than there are vacancies. But the maxim : "Reduce differentials !" is not by itself very helpful. What keeps the differentials artificially
high ? Is it government policy ? Surely not in all countries because in many
of them salaries are dominated by private firms? We are not going to make
much progress here unless we find out much more than we now know about
the hiring practices of both the private and the public sector in less developed
countries. Thus, labour market studies ought to be the kernel of the research
work of the World Employment Programme.[1]

A TRANSITORY PROBLEM ?

We know that unemployment in poor countries is at present concentrated
among the young and that even among them it is concentrated in the early
years of their working lives. Is this the invariant pattern or can we expect the
high rates of unemployment at present observed in the younger age groups to
become characteristic of the older age groups in time to come ? In other words,
will it always be largely youth unemployment and hence educated unemploy-

---

[1] And so it is : see ILO : *Scope, approach and content of research-oriented activities of the
World Employment Programme*, op. cit., p. 73.

ment, simply because in a rapidly growing educational system it is the young who receive the bulk of the additional education, or will it gradually turn into mass unemployment evenly distributed throughout all ages and all levels of education ? This is the critical question for the developing world.

To attempt a decisive answer to the question would be presumptuous. But a stab at an answer would run as follows : if the less developed countries maintain their present growth rates, the problem in the foreseeable future will indeed remain that of unemployment heavily concentrated among those aged 15 to 25. On the other hand, there is no easy remedy in sight for youth unemployment and for educated unemployment. The present tendency of educational systems to grow more quickly at the top rather than at the bottom of the educational ladder must somehow be reversed, and I have argued that this can be achieved only by a restructured pattern of educational finance combined with deliberate intervention in labour markets. But to reverse these trends does mean that we shall cure educated unemployment only to create or to aggravate the "school leaver problem". But the remedy for the school leaver problem, at least in the short run, lies in the provision of out-of-school education. In the long run, it lies in the slow and patient reform of primary education from within by curriculum reform, examination reform and the improvement of teacher training. It may not be a very exciting prospect for those who hanker for quick results, convinced that there is somewhere a clever idea never previously considered which will solve all our difficulties overnight. But here, as elsewhere, it is "piecemeal social engineering" which I believe will prove to be the method by which we shall eventually solve the problem.